Modesty

a Matter of the Heart

by Kathy L. Murray

If you are encouraged by this book and would like to help make it available to others, please mail your love offering to the address below. All that you give will go directly toward printing additional copies. Thank you for laboring together with us to reach and teach souls for Christ and his glory.

Ministering Seed to the Sower / <u>MODESTY BOOK</u>
1333 Manna Way
North Pole, AK 99705
USA

Modesty a Matter of the Heart
Copyright © 2008 by Kathy L. Murray
ISBN 978-0-9815538-0-1

5,000 First printing January 2005
10,000 Second printing May 2007
Revised January 2008
5,000 Third printing February 2008

Published by: Ministering Seed to the Sower
                1333 Manna Way
                North Pole, AK 99705
                Email: ModestyBook@gmail.com

Not Sold for Profit
Donations appreciated
For your convenience, if you would like to give an offering through PayPal, you can designate your gift to Modestybook@gmail.com

The statutes of the LORD are right,
rejoicing the heart: the commandment of
the LORD is pure, enlightening the eyes.

Psalm 19:8

TABLE OF CONTENTS

ACKNOWLEDGMENTS

This book is a result of a ladies' class that I began teaching in Mississippi. Conversing by telephone with Dr. K. Daniel Fried, I shared how the Lord opened the door for the class and the difference it was making in the lives of the ladies attending. Having been burdened for some time about the decrease in modesty among God's people, Brother Fried suggested that I either record the lessons on tape or write them in book form. He hoped to have them in time to distribute at his Hope of Israel Conference—only eight weeks away!

Though the task seemed impossible, the Lord immediately began opening doors and supplying every need. From beginning to finish, this book was ready for printing in less than five weeks. Only God could have coordinated the efforts of all involved and enabled us to have it ready in time for the conference. Now that our labour is finished and the books are being distributed, the Lord's work will continue as he touches the hearts and lives of its readers.

I am confident that God will reward each one according to his labor. Nevertheless, he tells us to give honor to whom honor is due (Romans 13:7). Therefore I express my appreciation to Pat Cassidy who drew the illustrations in chapter six and spent many hours proofreading. Others who helped tremendously by proofing are: Fay Collins, Brother Dan Fried and his wife Rebecca, Lisa Gilliam, Julianne Hall, Patrick Honeycutt, Holly Ladnier, Laura Martus, Hazel Shelton, and Pastor Steve Bankhead, who has also been a constant encouragement and support. I have thanked God many times for placing me under his leadership. I'm also grateful for his sweet wife Carol who has been a wonderful example of modesty. She is a godly pastor's wife and mother – a jewel rarely found in our day! I am also grateful to Karen McAlister, Pastor Doug Duffett, Judy Schaefer, Jackie Englund, Joni Youngberg, Jane Hanson, and Sheri Tibbetts for offering their skills and time in proofing this second edition.

Deep gratitude goes to Brother Mark Herbstritt who operates The Stable Printing Ministry and graciously printed the first set of covers at no charge. His contribution has been a great help financially. Also, much appreciation goes to Pastor Don Williams of Believers Baptist Church, as well as each one who helped with the printing, collating, and binding.

My love and appreciation is also due to Mr. and Mrs. Bill Riddick, who graciously supplied me with a comfortable place to stay while working on this booklet, as well as on other occasions. Their hospitality and kindness have made me feel as though I were a part of their family. (Philippians 1:3).

During this time, I also had the privilege of sitting under the preaching of Charles McKinney, pastor of Jesus Christ Baptist Church in Ocean Springs, Mississippi. He is indisputably a man who loves lost sinners and faithfully preaches *book - chapter - and verse* to his congregation. The value and fruitfulness of this man's ministry is evident by the degree of maturity seen in his flock.

Last but not least, most deserving of gratitude is my Saviour. Had not the Lord Jesus Christ saved me from sin and made me a new creature, I would not be concerned about modesty in the least—in my life or anyone else's. I thank God for the difference that knowing the Lord has made!

Kathy L. Murray

Introduction

There has never been a time when the plea for biblical modesty was more needed than in these last days of apostasy. We are seeing an epidemic of promiscuity among our youth. Adultery, fornication, and the like is largely a result of many brethren lowering the biblical standards of modesty, especially as seen among our ladies. We are living in a very licentious, wanton, and loose society which the enemies of God have orchestrated to seduce, tempt, and entice godly men and boys away from holy living. We are exhorted to abstain from all appearance of evil and from fleshly lusts which war against the soul. It is increasingly more difficult for our men and boys to keep pure minds. Immodestly dressed women are on billboards, television, the internet, and on magazine and book covers at the checkout isle. But the real tragedy is that this corruption is being displayed in so-called "Baptist" churches and "Christian" homes across the nation.

Churches are conforming to worldly standards at a rapid pace. Many are allowing the protective wall of godly apparel to be broken down, which was designed to protect us from provoking the sinful appetites of the heart. Historically, Baptist churches have exemplified godly standards of modesty. If we do not defend and protect that godly heritage, standards will continue decreasing within our churches.

As our world continues down the path of ungodliness, by the grace of God, we can continue to be the salt of the earth – the salt of humility, the salt of godliness, the salt of holy living, the salt of biblical modesty. Our good friend in the Lord, Sister Kathy Armentrout, has been burdened by God to set forth an encouraging treatise for all Christian ladies. Her premise is built on the Holy Scriptures, and we join her desire to provoke many to return to biblical standards of modesty, against the backdrop of a ungodly society. This book touches the HEART of the problem - that is, the HEARTS of God's people. Every Christian lady, teenager, and girl should be encouraged to read this very practical and helpful book. May God add His richest blessings and exhortation to all who read its message. Each word written comes from a meek and quiet spirit which desires only the best for us all. I commend our sister, her writing ministry, and her godly example to all the churches.

Dr. K. Daniel Fried, Director
Hope of Israel Baptist Mission

Chapter 1

The Joy of Salvation

*Therefore with joy shall ye draw water out of
the wells of salvation.* Isaiah 12:3

Just because people smile does not mean they are happy.
In this modern society, women in all walks of life are fighting
depression. There are thousands each year who succeed in
ending their lives. Suicide has crossed the minds of numerous
others, though they have not attempted it. Still others go from
day to day doing the best they know how, yet they lack joy and
purpose in life. One may face problems with money, family,
or health, while another is healthy, wealthy, or even popular.
But both of these have an emptiness within that is eating at
them like a disease.

Some try the "positive attitude" approach. Yet still, deep down
something is missing. As pain medicine may mask the root cause
without curing the problem, so pretending that all is well only
covers the deep-seated misery within. It will not cure the cause.
Not knowing how to change things, they try to conceal the pain;
but it's still there, gnawing at them. "Why am I here? Isn't there
more to life than this?" If you are asking that question, the answer
is, "Yes," there is more—much more!

We may look at the busy woman who has hobbies, a career, or
any number of daily activities that seem to fulfill her. But unless
she has the joy of the Lord her happiness is only *conditional.*
As soon as her circumstances change, her happiness level does
too. Her smile disappears, her goals suddenly seem beyond
reach, and she feels terribly alone. No longer able to pretend,
she sees the misery of her own soul as she looks in the mirror.
The truth is, underneath the smiles and behind the veil of her
heart is an emptiness that can only be filled by God.

The depression and heaviness which people feel cannot be removed by accumulating material possessions, achieving great accomplishments, being popular, taking antidepressants, or filling their days with entertainment. If you sense an emptiness in your life, it is not there because of something you need to obtain or accomplish. It is a spiritual void that needs to be filled. The emptiness within us can only be satisfied by our Creator. The Bible plainly tells us that all mankind is born separated from God because of *sin*. Like a chain, sin binds the human heart. There is only one sure hope of freedom—Jesus our Saviour. Salvation means freedom from sin and its shame and possessing the power to walk in joyful obedience with the Lord.

If you are wondering, "What do joy and salvation have to do with modesty?" Well, modesty, as well as many other good traits, will be the result of a heart that is right with God. The Bible says, "For as he thinketh in his heart, so is he..." Proverbs 23:7. Since our hearts govern our lives, it is beneficial that we take a good, honest look at this very important part of our being. Hearts are bound by sin, and sin destroys lives. This is why Jesus came: "To open their [our] eyes and to turn them *[us]* from darkness to light, and from the power of Satan unto God, that they [we] may receive forgiveness of sins, and inheritance among them which are sanctified by faith that is in me [Jesus]." Acts 26:18. "For he hath looked down from the height of his sanctuary; from heaven did the LORD behold the earth; To hear the groaning of the prisoner; to loose *[set free]* those that are appointed to death." Psalm 102:19, 20. Jesus came to set us free that we might walk with him in the way of righteousness.

Access to this path is not obtained by our own efforts. Belonging to a church, the prayers of others, doing good deeds, or being born into a religious family will not save you from your sin. No church, friend, or family member can obtain salvation for you. "None of them can by any means redeem his brother, nor give to God a ransom for him." Psalm 49:7. Neither can any man obtain salvation for himself. "Not by works of righteousness which we have done, but according to his mercy he saved us..." Titus 3:5. The Lord Jesus Christ is the only way to have peace with God the Father. Salvation was obtained and made available to us when Jesus shed his blood for our sins. His work on the cross satisfied the wrath of God and forever opened the door so that we may dwell with Him. It is important to know that you cannot trust your own works or religion while trusting Christ for salvation. Your faith must be in Christ. Jesus alone is "the door" as well as the guide along this glorious pathway. He said, "I am the door: by me if any man enter in, he shall be saved..." John 10:9. The Lord made the way easy to understand. You simply need to believe God. Although God desires that everyone walk with him in the paths of righteousness, only those individuals who are willing to turn to God and trust Christ for the forgiveness of sins will be saved. Please make sure you are saved! It is only through Jesus that one may experience having eternal peace with God. Oh, what joy there is in *knowing* that you are saved!

Temporal happiness versus lasting joy

One of the greatest truths a person can understand is that temporal happiness and lasting joy are not the same. Temporal happiness comes from relationships, money, or circumstances of life being in our favor. This is very different from possessing the true and lasting joy which comes from God alone. Happiness is conditional, but true joy is unconditional. In Christ, we have a deep-seated joy that will endure unsettling changes in our temporal circumstances. Genuine joy comes from knowing the Lord. But before one can know the Lord, that individual must first take an honest look at his or her own heart and realize their need of Christ.

We must see ourselves and our sins for what they truly are in God's sight. When people are honest with themselves, they know deep down that their lives are not what they should be. Some, who recognize their sinfulness try to correct the problem

7

themselves by making minor changes in the way they live. Many even become devout church members (and others, church leaders) conforming to certain acts that they consider religious. They are desperately trying to ease their guilty consciences by doing good works. But their attempts to feel acceptable to God are vain and will never grant them forgiveness or peace. Sadly, all they have is an *outward* conformity covering the emptiness and sin within. It is vain *religion they have*, not a life-giving *relationship* with God. Many mistakenly consider themselves Christians because they are familiar with Christian terminology, have memorized some Bible verses, or have prayed a prayer repeating someone else's words. These sincere, yet lost people have a head knowledge that has never reached their hearts. They are hoping that by living a religious or good life they will somehow earn favor with God. To think this way shows a lack of understanding concerning salvation. The penalty of sin is death and we are helplessness to save ourselves. Christ's sacrifice made for every man's sin is complete and the only payment God will accept. Do you *trust the blood* that Jesus shed for your sins, or are you *trying to earn* God's favor?

Religion or Relationship?

According to the word of God, many sincerely religious people will stand before Him on that great Day of Judgment— *religious*, but without a personal *relationship* with God. Jesus said, "Not every one that saith unto me, Lord, Lord, shall enter into the kingdom of heaven; but he that doeth the will of my Father which is in heaven. Many will say to me in that day, Lord, Lord, have we not done many wonderful works? And then will I profess unto them, I never knew you: depart from me, ye that work iniquity." Matthew 7:21-23. It amazes me that people like those spoken of in this passage go to hell after working in the name of Jesus. They were not drunkards, adulterers, or idol worshipers. They were sincerely doing many good deeds in Jesus' name, but they were without Christ as their Saviour. Likewise, many today trust their own deeds rather than the

8

blood of Christ to pardon their sins. Imagine dying, lifting your eyes up in hell, and not realizing until then, that you had trusted your good works instead of Jesus' blood. How horrible to die without Christ, thinking you were saved! The Bible exhorts, "Examine yourselves, whether ye be in the faith; prove your own selves…" II Corinthians 13:5. Sincerity will not get a person to heaven. Many people are sincere, but they are sincerely wrong. It is God's way or no way! My friend, salvation is received by faith in Christ, not by religious acts. To escape hell and go to heaven, you must *know* the Lord, and he must know you. To *know* denotes a personal relationship.

For instance, the media is full of information about our President. I can tell you a lot *about* him, yet I do not *know* him personally. If I met the President on the street, he would not know me! Unlike our President, God is not a mere man. He already knows everything about you, but that does not mean you have a relationship with him. He fashioned you in your mother's womb and gives you each breath you take (Psalm 139). He knows every sin you have or ever will commit. He knows those things you refuse to admit about yourself. But, to be acknowledged by him, you must have a personal relationship with him.

The first step to having joy and peace is true salvation. This means to be reconciled to God having your sins forgiven and your heart changed by a power higher than yourself – by the grace of Almighty God. Salvation is through faith in Christ, not our own works. "For he that is entered into his rest, he also hath ceased from his own works…" Hebrews 4:10. "For by grace are ye saved through faith; and that not of yourselves: it is the gift of God: Not of works, lest any man should boast." Ephesians 2:8, 9.

Is it the shed blood of Christ you are trusting, or are you hoping that your good deeds outweigh your bad? For your soul's sake, please understand that it doesn't work that way. One day, a multitude following Jesus asked him, "What shall we do, that we might work the works of God?" Jesus answered, "This is the work of God, that ye believe on him whom he hath sent." John 6:28, 29.

9

God's thoughts or my thoughts?

In God's word we find written, "For my thoughts are not your thoughts, neither are your ways my ways, saith the LORD. For as the heavens are higher than the earth, so are my ways higher than your ways, and my thoughts than your thoughts." Isaiah 55:8, 9. It is dangerous to assume that God thinks the same way we do. For instance, it may seem logical to us that lying is not as bad as murder—or is it? How many times does a murderer have to kill before he is called a murderer? Only once, right? Now, how many times does a person have to lie before he is known to be a liar? The earliest lie I remember telling was on my first day of kindergarten. How about you? Have you made it this far without ever lying? Surely not. Lies may seem small if we compare them to the murders of a serial killer, but God does not compare your sin or mine with anyone else's. He sees all sin in light of his holy law. The same God who said, "Thou shalt not kill," also said, "Ye shall not steal, neither deal falsely, neither lie one to another." Leviticus 19:11. Furthermore, God has decreed that all liars will go to the same eternal hell as murderers! "But the fearful, and unbelieving, and the abominable, and murderers, and whoremongers, and sorcerers, and idolaters, **and all liars**, shall have their part in the lake that burneth with fire and brimstone..." Revelation 21:8.

God does not think as man thinks. The law of God was given to reveal his holy and righteous character, and he will never change. When we see our conduct in the light of his perfect law, we are able to understand that we fall short and deserve punishment. "For the wages of sin is death…" Romans 6:23. None of us are exempt, "For all have sinned, and come short of the glory of God." Romans 3:23. Our sins against God are *not* a light thing! Sin brings the justifiable wrath of God upon the individual who has committed even one. Lying, cursing, immodesty, fornication, pornography, adultery, etc., may be thought of as "little" sins and excused by man. But just because we excuse them does not mean that they are excused by

God. If we shrug off sin in our lives as "no big deal," we have dangerously failed to understand God's holiness, righteousness, and coming judgment.

Our society is lacking a good healthy fear of God and needs to know that ignorance of God's truth will not excuse them in the end. The scriptures say, "It is a fearful thing to fall into the hands of the living God." Hebrews 10:31. "But I will forewarn you whom ye shall fear: Fear him, which after he hath killed hath power to cast into hell; yea, I say unto you, Fear him." Luke 12:5. Friend, if you do not know the Lord and continue on without Christ as your personal Saviour, you will one day meet God as your all-knowing and righteous Judge. The wisest choice a sinner can make is to repent and fall at the feet of God, receiving the mercy that is offered him through Christ.

God the Father could have done nothing and rightfully sent us to hell for sinning against him. Jesus was not obligated to die in our place so that we could be forgiven. But God chose to love us and judged his own Son in our place, and he has promised salvation to all who put their faith in Christ. As a leopard cannot change his own spots, neither can we deliver ourselves from our sins and their penalty. It is worth saying again, *our only hope is that our sins be forgiven*, and there is only **one** payment God will accept—the blood of his Son Jesus Christ. Deliverance is possible by the power and grace of God. Jesus has already shed his pure and precious blood for you. God the Father showed the world that he accepted that payment when he resurrected his Son from the dead! Jesus has finished his work of redemption and now sits at the right hand of the throne of God (Hebrews 12:2).

You will never be able to know and serve the Lord until you humbly receive salvation by God's grace, admitting you are neither worthy nor able to merit your own. If you know beyond any doubt that you are saved, I rejoice with you! If not, please do not harden your heart or let the devil deceive you any longer. You must turn to the Lord. Believe that he will save you the moment you rest your soul on the finished work of Christ.

The salvation testimony of Albert Benjamin Simpson.
1843-1919

While glancing through the library of his former minister and tutor, Albert Simpson came across an old musty volume called <u>Marshall's Gospel Mystery of Sanctification</u>. As he scanned its pages, a sentence which opened the gates of life eternal caught his eye:

'The first good work you will ever perform is to believe on the Lord Jesus Christ. Until you do this, all your works, prayers, tears, and good resolutions are vain. To believe on the Lord Jesus is just to believe that he saves you according to his word, that he receives and saves you here and now, for he has said – 'Him that cometh to me I will in no wise cast out.'

He fell to his knees and cried out to the Lord Jesus to save him: 'I come the best I can, and I dare to believe that Thou doest receive me and save me, and that I am now Thy child, forgiven and saved simply because I have taken Thee at Thy word.'

Regardless of how you've lived your life, the blood of Jesus Christ was shed for all of your sins. His blood is pure and sufficient to cleanse you completely. "But this man, after he had offered one sacrifice for sins forever, sat down on the right hand of God;" Hebrews 10:12. The word of God says, "For whosoever shall call upon the name of the Lord shall be saved." Romans 10:13. That *whosoever* includes you! Don't gamble with your soul. The Bible says, "...now is the accepted time; behold, now is the day of salvation." II Corinthians 6:2. Have you called upon the Lord, trusting Christ?

Only by God's grace do we have the power to walk with and serve the Lord. (see II Timothy 1:9). Our desire is that "the God of hope fill you with all joy and peace in believing..." Romans 15:13. If you have asked the Lord to save you, he promised, "...I will never leave thee, nor forsake thee." Hebrews 13:5. "And I give unto them eternal life; and they shall never perish..." John 10:28.

The beginning of wisdom

The fear of the LORD is the beginning of wisdom: and the knowledge of the holy is understanding. Proverbs 9:10

Once we become children of God, it is imperative that we guard our minds from the ungodly thinking of this world. With reverence for God decreasing rapidly in our day, it is necessary to address a false notion that is influencing even the hearts of God's people. God is not "the man upstairs"; nor is he our "good ol' buddy" that we need no longer fear. To them who do not fear him, the Lord said, "Hear now this, O foolish people, and without understanding; which have eyes, and see not; which have ears, and hear not: Fear ye not me? saith the LORD: will ye not tremble at my presence...?" Jeremiah 5:21, 22. It will help to bear in mind that it was God who destroyed Sodom and Gomorrah for their sin and drowned his enemies in the Red Sea; and to all mankind today he has proclaimed, "For I am the LORD, I change not..." Malachi 3:6. Jesus himself displayed the righteous anger of God when he turned over tables and seats while driving religious hypocrites from the temple (Matthew 21:12, 13). As he did this, he quoted the word of God, exposing their sin and reminding them that the right priority in the house of God is prayer. (I cannot continue without saying that I am greatly saddened by the priority of most churches in our day. Many are thought of as places of entertainment and social activities, such as sports, plays, gospel sings, dinners, carnivals, etc. It is certainly easier and more pleasant to have social activities in the name of evangelism than it is to acknowledge our sin and repent, to fast, weep, and pray, asking God for grace to live for his glory, and for souls to be saved (see II Chronicles 7:14)).

As children of God, we no longer have to fear the eternal, justifiable wrath of God. The Lord Jesus willingly endured the wrath we deserve. Nevertheless, we should most assuredly fear our loving Father's chastening hand. Just as a good earthly father chastens his offspring, so the Lord chastens his children when we disobey him. "For they verily for a few days chastened us after their own pleasure; but he for our profit, that we might be partakers of his holiness." Hebrews 12:10. The Lord knows where we are in our spiritual walk, and he knows what we need to learn. As his dear children, we are privileged to know him as our compassionate Saviour, guiding Shepherd, faithful Friend, and all-knowing Father. He loves us with an everlasting love—yet, he is still Almighty God. He is to be reverenced and obeyed!

Thank God for his long-suffering, but there are occasions when God's judgment is swift and without opportunity for repentance. In Acts, chapter 5, the Lord could have dealt gently with Ananias and Sapphira, but gentleness was not the message he intended for the church. The power of God was displayed when this man and his wife dropped dead for lying to the Holy Ghost. "And great fear came upon all the church, and upon as many as heard these things." Acts 5:11. The Lord loves his children, but he has purposed that we be partakers of his holiness (Hebrews 12:10). Wise are those children who fear his chastening hand! "For whom the Lord loveth he chasteneth..." Hebrews 12:6. For those who think of God as nothing more than a big, cushy teddy bear, they should consider John's experience on the Isle of Patmos. "And when I saw him, I fell at his feet as dead..." Revelation 1:17. There was something about seeing the Lord Jesus Christ glorified and exalted that caused John to fall at his feet as dead! Although God humbled himself to redeem, care for, and commune with us, his creation, we should not fail to be aware of who he is in position and power!

Saved and Full of Joy

Maybe you are a young Christian and have not yet learned the wonderful benefits of being saved. If so, your joy will increase as you learn and obey the Lord's word and his will for your life. If you have been saved for some time but have not followed the Lord as you should, there are surely consequences for not doing so. Understanding a few things that affect our joy will help us to possess and experience the abundant life promised to us by God.

14

- <u>There is joy in knowing the LORD</u>: "These things have I written unto you that believe on the name of the Son of God; that ye may know that ye have eternal life…" I John 5:13. "Yet I will rejoice in the LORD, I will joy in the God of my salvation." Habakkuk 3:18.

- <u>Walking close to the Lord brings joy</u>: "Thou wilt shew me the path of life: in thy presence is fulness of joy; at thy right hand there are pleasures forevermore." Psalm 16:11.

- <u>Sin can rob us of joy</u>: After David repented of his sin concerning Bathsheba, he prayed, "Restore unto me the joy of thy salvation…" Psalm 51:12.

- <u>Answered prayer brings joy</u>: Jesus said, "Hitherto have ye asked nothing in my name: ask, and ye shall receive, that your joy may be full." John 16:24.

- <u>Joy is the reward of right living</u>: "For God giveth to a man that is good in his sight wisdom, and knowledge, and joy: but to the sinner he giveth travail,…" Ecclesiastes 2:26.

- <u>Being meek will cause our joy to increase</u>: "The meek also shall increase their joy in the LORD…" Isaiah 29:19.

A Christian can have peace *with* God (salvation) yet not have the peace *of* God, which comes when we yield to his will. Our mind may tell us that we need this or that to make us happy. We strive to obtain something only to find that we still are not satisfied. Why is this so? Because, our purpose in life is not to seek our own happiness or pleasure, but rather to seek God's will and his glory. Only by doing the will of God will we find the fulfillment for which we have been searching.

What about my plans, my hopes, and my dreams? "For the LORD God is a sun and shield: the LORD will give grace and glory: no good thing will he withhold from them that walk uprightly." Psalm 84:11. If you are walking uprightly and your desire is good, the Lord will not withhold your request. Though a child does not always understand, his parent may withhold a request to keep him from sorrow or danger. As God's child, do you always know or want that which is best for you? Walking by faith means trusting God in the smallest matters, including what he does or does not allow in your life.

In conclusion

It is impossible for you to be all that God created you to be until you are first reconciled to him. God's righteousness is freely given to us the moment we receive Christ as our Saviour. Are you saved? After salvation, if we are going to walk more perfectly with the Lord, we must make it our daily priority to learn more of him. The life of a Christian is a constant learning experience. It is our responsibility as children of God to *walk* in his righteousness in order to rightly represent him in this world. Our joy will become more abundant as we learn, yield to, and experience the Lord's will for our lives. We are saved from sin and its penalty to serve our Lord.

There is no room for complacency in his children. The Lord said, "Follow me." Those who know him follow him, for he said, "My sheep hear my voice, and I know them, and they follow me: And I give unto them eternal life; and they shall never perish, neither shall any man pluck them out of my hand." John 10:27, 28.

To follow the Lord you must get up, leave the sin and weights behind, and set your eyes on Jesus (Hebrews 12:1-2). Following the Lord takes determination, effort, and purpose of heart. Those that have excelled in the world have been individuals who refused to accept defeat or spend their time looking back. In Christianity, no man or woman has ever become a great asset to the kingdom of God by being complacent. Hebrews, chapter 11 proclaims the testimonies of men and women who knew the Lord and followed him, whatever the cost.

Contrary to the world's views, success is not measured by one's activity level, popularity, social status, or any such thing; but rather, it is determined by the extent to which one is yielded to and used of God for his purposes. To be successful in God's eyes, we must walk with him by faith. As we study and obey God's word, we will walk with his leading and accomplish his will, his way. After instructing his disciples, Jesus said, "If ye know these things, *happy* are ye if ye do them." John 13:17. Oh, that each of God's children would experience the joy of the Lord which comes from living in obedience to his will.

Chapter 2

The Rewards of Seeking Him

Glory ye in his holy name: let the heart of them rejoice that seek the LORD. Seek the LORD and his strength, seek his face continually. I Chronicles 16:10, 11

What a blessing it is to be reconciled to God, brought back into a right relationship with our creator. Not only are we saved from the punishment we deserve, which is eternal separation from God in the lake of fire, but we are given new life, eternal life. Knowing that you are saved from hell and having the promise of heaven are wonderful, but salvation is so much more. Having eternal life is directly related to *knowing* God. "And this is life eternal, <u>that they might know thee the only true God,</u> and Jesus Christ, whom thou hast sent." John 17:3. As his children we are exhorted to "…seek his face continually."

"O the depth of the riches both of the wisdom and knowledge of God! how unsearchable are his judgments, and his ways past finding out!" (Romans 11:33). If we dedicated the remainder of our days to learning the heart of God, all of our acquired knowledge might equal one grain of sand in contrast to the vast amount of wisdom there is to be known. Yet, every grain of knowledge that we acquire of the Lord is as a pearl of great price. Once obtained and its worth realized, we are compelled to seek to know him more. What riches are to be had! Riches free for the taking, and he bids us, "Come unto me" and "learn of me." Matthew 11:28, 29.

Understanding the heart of God

Sadly, one of the greatest atrocities of our day is the number of Christians who are ignorantly misrepresenting God. Realizing this, I have been asking the Lord to reveal himself more clearly to me. I desire to understand his ways so that, with my life, I do not misrepresent him to others. To the degree that each of us is conformed to the image of Christ, we are like God (godly). Any area we are unlike Christ, we are <u>ungodly</u> in our actions. Christians are called to be like Christ. "For whom he did foreknow, he also did predestinate to be conformed to the image of his Son..." Romans 8:29.

DEF. *Image*: A representation or similitude of any person or thing; an idea; a representation of any thing to the mind; a conception. Thus, a mirror reflects the image of a person standing before it. (Noah Webster's 1828 Dictionary)

The Lord understands that we are flesh, but we are not without God's grace and power. Peter said, "According as his divine power hath given unto us all things that pertain unto life and godliness, through the knowledge of him that hath called us to glory and virtue." II Peter 1:3. We have God's word at our fingertips and his grace is freely offered. Therefore we have no excuse for walking ignorantly of his will and remaining unlearned. Our daily goal should be to learn more of him. Whether in word or deed, we should be careful as to how we represent him to others. The more we are conformed to the image of Christ, the more accurately we will represent our Lord and bring him glory in this present world (see Titus 2:12).

As any relationship takes effort so does knowing more of the Lord. He bestows knowledge of himself unto all who seek; and all who seek will find and be abundantly blessed. The Lord sees every heart, and his eye is on those who seek to know him more perfectly. He referred to David as such a man. "...I have found David the son of Jesse, <u>a man after mine own heart</u>, <u>which</u> shall fulfil <u>all</u> <u>my</u> <u>will</u>." Acts 13:22. David persistently longed to know the Lord and obediently fulfill God's will. Any man or woman who desires to please the Lord will diligently seek to know God's heart.

Men so desired the wisdom and understanding that the Lord had imparted to King Solomon that they sought out and copied his proverbs (Proverbs 25:1). Do we desire wisdom so fervently?

Seeking God with your whole heart.

As the hart panteth after the water brooks,
so panteth my soul after thee, O God. Psalm 42:1.

Notice the action verbs in the following verses. "My son, if thou wilt <u>receive</u> my words, and <u>hide</u> my commandments with thee; So that thou <u>incline</u> thine ear unto wisdom, and <u>apply</u> thine heart to understanding; Yea, if thou <u>criest</u> after knowledge, and <u>liftest</u> up thy voice for understanding; If thou <u>seekest</u> her as silver, and <u>searchest</u> for her as for hid treasures; Then shalt thou understand the fear of the LORD, and <u>find</u> the knowledge of God. For the LORD <u>giveth</u> wisdom: out of his mouth <u>cometh</u> knowledge and understanding." Proverbs 2:1-6. Did you notice the last two action verbs are God's action? When we get serious about seeking him, he responds by <u>giving</u> us what we need. "<u>Draw nigh to God, and he will draw nigh to you</u>. Cleanse your hands, ye sinners; and purify your hearts, ye double minded." James 4:8.

One man that was not so pleasing to God was King Abijam who reigned over Judah. The Bible says, "Three years reigned he in Jerusalem. And his mother's name was Maachah, the daughter of Abishalom. And he walked in all the sins of his father, which he had done before him: <u>and his heart was not perfect with the LORD his God,</u> as the heart of David his father." I Kings 15:2, 3. Maybe King Abijam said the same thing I often hear repeated in our day, "Nobody's perfect. God will overlook my failures." It is true that as long as we are in these mortal bodies, we cannot live without sinning, but this does not excuse our lack of effort to walk perfectly before God each day (I John 2:6). "Be ye therefore perfect, even as your Father which is in heaven is perfect." Matthew 5:48.

Would the Lord Jesus command us to do something that is not possible? Of course not. Being perfect does not mean that you'll never fail God again. It simply means walking in obedience to that which God has shown you thus far. It denotes maturity. When one has a mature attitude, that person will readily receive instruction and apply it without resistance. If I am not obeying the Lord in any area that He has revealed truth to me, my heart is not perfect with him. The moment I yield to him in that area, my heart is once again perfect with the Lord. When he puts his finger on something else in my life, I choose to yield or resist. How I respond will determine whether or not I continue walking perfectly before him. We cannot walk with a perfect heart while resisting God's will in even the smallest point.

How important is seeking God to you?

Draw nigh to God,
and he will draw nigh to you... James 4:8

Our priorities show who or what is important to us. If the Lord is important, we will make it a point to draw near to him. This may mean getting out of bed early to pray and read his word. If we do, the rewards will far surpass the small sacrifice we make. Yes, sleep is a blessing and needed, but do we love sleep so much that we will choose it over spending time with our Lord?

How many of us started out on fire for God and years later realized that we lost our zeal? We are flesh, and the world is constantly pulling at our affections. Are we aware of the danger of drifting away from the things of God? Revelation, chapter 3, reminds us of the consequences of losing our first love. If we have allowed ourselves to leave our first love and realize the seriousness of the problem, we will do something about it. The remedy for our condition is found in Revelation 2:5, "Remember therefore from whence thou art fallen, and repent...." We have too many promises of God to excuse ourselves for remaining in a backslidden condition. If we cultivate a heart like Job's, God's word will be more important to us than our necessary food (Job 23:12). Only then will we receive the nourishment, strength, and wisdom needed to live a victorious life. If we are ever going to help others know the Lord, we are going to have to make it a priority of knowing him ourselves.

Humility is a must!

...be clothed with humility: for God resisteth the proud, and giveth grace to the humble. I Peter 5:5

As Bible truths of modesty and other Christian principles are learned and applied, it is not uncommon for an immature Christian to develop a high-minded spirit. The scriptures speak of a novice (a new Christian) as being susceptible to pride (1 Timothy 3:6). This is because he or she learns many doctrinal truths, but does not yet understand the humility of Christ necessary to deliver or display them properly.

One of the world's greatest needs is examples of godly women. Our church families and communities need women who are REAL and HUMBLE. We need women who desire to live godly lives, yet willing to admit they have areas of needed growth. That takes honesty. If we live before others as though we have "arrived," we will never have a moment's peace. Why? Because we would be putting all of our energies into hiding our failures, instead of getting victory over them. It is vital for you and me to be teachable, and the best place to begin is by being honest with ourselves. Even if we have been saved and serving the Lord for many years, there is still plenty of room to grow in grace and knowledge of our Lord—to walk more perfectly with him (II Peter 3:18).

We display a froward heart when we excuse ungodliness with the attitude, "This is who I am, take me or leave me. I'm not going to change." Any one with this kind of attitude does not have a gracious and teachable spirit. The Bible tells us, "A gracious woman retaineth honour..." Proverbs 11:16.

The Lord may use a preacher, teacher, friend, or any number of ways to reveal himself and his will to us, but the source and giver of truth is God himself. (It is important to remember that when God uses someone or something to confirm truth, it will never contradict his word, for his word is truth.) The Lord used an ass to speak to Balaam, a lost woman to speak to Peter when he denied Christ, Stephen to speak to an unyielding crowd, Paul to speak to the church, and an angel to speak to John on the Isle of Patmos. Whatever or whoever he uses is up to him, but ultimately it is God who is speaking, and it is God who gives the increase. Paul said, "Who then is Paul, and who is Apollos, but ministers by whom ye believed, even as the Lord gave to every man? I have planted, Apollos watered; but God gave the increase. So then neither is he that planteth any thing, neither he that watereth; but God that giveth the increase." I Corinthians 3:5-7.

Then, there are the hearers. The Lord said, "A wise man will hear, and will increase learning..." Proverbs 1:5. Ladies, if we ever get to the place that we are not teachable, we have gotten too big for our corsets. "Reproofs of instruction are the way of life..." "...but fools despise wisdom and instruction." Proverbs 6:23; 1:7. No one is humble unless they are approachable and teachable. A teachable spirit is a meek spirit. "Good and upright is the LORD: therefore will he teach sinners in the way. The meek will he guide in judgment: and the meek will he teach his way." Psalm 25:8, 9.

DEF. *Meek*: Appropriately humble, in an evangelical sense; submissive to the divine will; not proud, self-sufficient or refractory. (Noah Webster's 1828 Dictionary)

We are constantly exhorted in scripture to "Be of the same mind one toward another. Mind not high things, but condescend to men of low estate. Be not wise in your own conceits." Romans 12:16. Successful Christian living takes daily walking in the grace of God. Humility is a must. The Lord will purposely resist a proud doer, and he or she will not prosper spiritually. "...God resisteth the proud, but giveth grace unto the humble." James 4:6. If we have a teachable spirit, we will continue growing as we seek to know the heart of the Lord.

So how do I seek the Lord?

When thou saidst, Seek ye my face; my heart said unto thee,
Thy face, LORD, will I seek. Psalm 27:8

Seeking the Lord is not difficult. It simply takes desire put into action. Here is how we can know the Lord better:

1. The word of God. Jesus said, "<u>Search the scriptures</u>; for in them ye think ye have eternal life: and <u>they are they which testify of me</u>." John 5:39. Has reading God's word become drudgery to you? Do you find your mind wandering as you flip through its pages? We have all been there, but none of us has to stay in that awful state of mind. There is so much more than stories, principles, and doctrine in that wonderful Book. God's word is where we find Jesus, who is eager to lead us into *all* truth.

Notice the wonderful truths found in Psalm 23. It is impossible for those who are without Christ to understand the full teaching of this shepherd's Psalm. Even more sadly, many Christians rarely consider its poetic words as anything other than a comforting passage for those who have lost a loved one. The LORD truly is our death bed Comforter; but before death, he is our Shepherd through life. This moment and each moment of every day "…he leadeth me in the paths of righteousness for his name's sake." Have you somehow forgotten that the great Shepherd of the sheep is *your* Shepherd? The Spirit of the Lord uses his word to guide us. Therefore, we need to remind ourselves often of how important our Shepherd's word is to our lives.

The word of God is our…

> <u>Comfort and hope.</u> "For whatsoever things were written aforetime were written for our learning, that we through patience and comfort of the scriptures might have hope." Romans 15:4 "Remember the word unto thy servant, upon which thou hast caused me to hope." Psalm 119:49.

Spiritual nourishment. "...It is written, That man shall not live by bread alone, but by every word of God." Luke 4:4.

Source of instruction. "Apply thine heart unto instruction, and thine ears to the words of knowledge." Proverbs 23:12.

Guide to living a clean life. "Wherewithal shall a young man cleanse his way? by taking heed thereto according to thy word." Psalm 119:9.

Light in a dark world. "Thy word is a lamp unto my feet, and a light unto my path." Psalm 119:105.

Judge. Jesus said, "He that rejecteth me, and receiveth not my words, hath one that judgeth him: the word that I have spoken, the same shall judge him in the last day." John 12:48.

The importance that God places on his word can be understood by observing how severely he deals with those who disregard it: "Seeing thou hatest instruction, and castest my words behind thee...and I kept silence; thou thoughtest that I was altogether such an one as thyself: but I will reprove thee, and set them in order before thine eyes.... " Psalm 50:17, 21. Speaking to those who are not listening to his words, God says, "Will ye not receive instruction to hearken to my word? saith the LORD." Jeremiah 35:13. "Turn you at my reproof: behold, I will pour out my spirit unto you, I will make known my words unto you." Proverbs 1:23.

The more we love God and search his word, the more we will understand his ways. No one can worship the Lord "in truth" unless they are walking in the light of his word. Walking in truth is so important that it is a prerequisite to answered prayer. "The LORD is nigh unto all them that call upon him, to all that call upon him in truth." Psalm 145:18. Are you walking in light of God's word?

25

He heareth the prayer of the righteous. Proverbs 15:29

2. Prayer. Time and time again the Lord bids us to pray. We sometimes neglect to give ourselves to prayer. We act as though he were asking us to take out the trash or do some unsavory task. Child of God, he is asking us to spend time with him, which will benefit us and others immensely. I present to you only a few of the many benefits that should motivate us to pray. Through our prayers our Father will...

Keep us from temptation and evil. "Watch ye and pray, lest ye enter into temptation. The spirit truly is ready, but the flesh is weak." Teaching his disciples, Jesus said, "When ye pray, say …and lead us not into temptation; but deliver us from evil." Jabez prayed, "…and that thine hand might be with me, and that thou wouldest keep me from evil, that it may not grieve me! And God granted him that which he requested." Mark 14:38; Luke 11:2-4; I Chronicles 4:10.

Make us joyful. We become more aware of the realness of God in our lives when we know he has heard and answered a specific prayer. "Hitherto have ye asked nothing in my name: ask, and ye shall receive, that your joy may be full." John 16:24. "Even them will I bring to my holy mountain, and make them joyful in my house of prayer…" Isaiah 56:7.

Bestow upon us mercy and needed grace. "Let us therefore come boldly unto the throne of grace, that we may obtain mercy, and find grace to help in time of need." Hebrews 4:16.

Strengthen and help others. Jesus prayed for us in John, chapter 17. Paul prayed for the brethren in Ephesians 1:16-19; 3:14-19; and Colossians 1:9-11. Paul pleaded with the saints to remember him in prayer, knowing that he would be helped by God as a result (Romans 15:30; Philemon 1:22).

Answer our requests. "Ask, and it shall be given you; seek, and ye shall find; knock, and it shall be opened unto you: For every one that asketh receiveth; and he that seeketh findeth; and to him that knocketh it shall be opened." Matthew 7:7, 8.

The Lord said, "Ye lust, and have not: ye kill, and desire to have, and cannot obtain: ye fight and war, yet ye have not, because ye ask not." James 4:2. It is a wonderful thing when we stop looking to others for our needs and desires and start looking to God alone. If you take your request to him and it is good in his sight, he will grant what you ask. "And this is the confidence that we have in him, that, if we ask any thing according to his will, he heareth us: And if we know that he hear us, whatsoever we ask, we know that we have the petitions that we desired of him." I John 5:14, 15. If he does not answer right away, you can trust that he is indeed working, and his timing is always best.

If you are disappointed with the Lord's response to your prayers, the reason may be that you do not trust him or his timing as you should. We must be careful to pray, yield to God's will, and trust our Father's care for us. James wrote in chapter 4, "Ye ask, and receive not, because ye ask amiss, that ye may consume it upon your lusts." There is always good reason when the Lord does not give us what we ask for. Trust Him. He knows the end from the beginning.

Jesus was an example of submission to the Father's will. At that crucial hour before his crucifixion, he knelt in agonizing prayer. Though he struggled with the thought of what he was about to endure, he chose to yield himself to his Father's will and prayed, "Not my will but thine be done." Likewise, when we pray we should pray with a submissive, trustful heart toward our Father. Doing so will enable us to walk with an undisturbed peace that passes all understanding. Trustful prayer is a result of faith in our Father's watchful care for us, as well as those for whom we are praying.

Another noteworthy thought before going on, is the importance of our submission to whatever the Lord's answer may be. Last week, a friend gave me the following quote (author unknown): "When God closes a door, don't climb through the window." Be careful not to force things to happen your way. You may be extremely regretful once you get what you want! (Psalm 106:13-15). Pray in faith, rest in God's will, and trust him concerning timing.

And be ye thankful. Colossians 3:15

3. Thanksgiving and Praise. The definition of praise is an extensive study which we will not go into here. Nevertheless, it is important to mention that immodest behavior should not be excused in the name of praise. I have seen ladies who *thought* they were praising God in church, but in reality they were grossly dishonoring him. Their actions were immodest, their conduct unladylike, and their flesh in control. I've been in services where you could not possibly hear the word of God being preached because of a woman demanding the attention of the congregation through her "praise" of God. It is important to remember that God has magnified his "word above his name." (Psalm 138:2). It is his word that God uses to instruct, rebuke, and encourage his children, as well as save lost souls. For this reason, God is not pleased when anyone distracts from the preaching of his word. When true praise is exhibited, it will not turn everyone's eyes upon a person, it will turn every eye and heart to the Lord! Praise that glorifies God cannot be separated from modest or respectful behavior, especially in the presence of men in the house of God. If we are going to please the Lord, we must do *all* to His glory. A meek and quiet spirit is in the sight of God of great price. Rather than dishonor the Lord, a modest woman will show forth a thankful heart, magnify Christ instead of herself, and conduct herself in a manner which is becoming of a saint. The Lord is worthy of our praise throughout each day. Let us take a quick look at the importance of praise.

<u>Thanksgiving and praise in prayer.</u> "Enter into his gates with thanksgiving, and into his courts with praise: be thankful unto him, and bless his name." Psalm 100:4.

<u>Praise in song.</u> "Saying, I will declare thy name unto my brethren, in the midst of the church will I sing praise unto thee." "The LORD is my strength and my shield; my heart trusted in him, and I am helped: therefore my heart greatly rejoiceth; and with my song will I praise him." Hebrews 2:12; Psalm 28:7.

<u>Daily attitude of praise.</u> "By him therefore let us offer the sacrifice of praise to God continually, that is, the fruit of our lips, giving thanks to his name." Hebrews 13:15. "And let the peace of God rule in your hearts, to the which also ye are called in one body; and be ye thankful." Colossians 3:15.

Did you notice that praise is defined as giving thanks unto his name? "By him therefore let us offer the sacrifice of praise to God continually, that is, <u>the fruit of our lips, giving thanks to his name</u>." Hebrews 13:15. Praise is natural when we stop to remember where the Lord has brought us from and where we are going. The importance of what we think on is understood by the effect it has on our attitude toward God. You will never worship the Lord while harboring an ungrateful heart.

In that heavenly city we will be free from all tears, sickness, misunderstandings, persecutions, and distresses. Paul put it this way: "For our light affliction, which is but for a moment, worketh for us a far more exceeding and eternal weight of glory." II Corinthians 4:17. "For I reckon that the sufferings of this present time are not worthy to be compared with the glory which shall be revealed in us." Romans 8:18. Truths like these give us hope and strength as we meditate upon them instead of our circumstances (Philippians 4:6-8).

Several years ago, I found myself overwhelmed by circumstances and very discouraged. I picked up a notebook and began writing down a few of God's blessings and answers to prayer. Very little paper had been used before my attitude changed dramatically. It is amazing what a thankful heart will do for us! We may not be able to change our circumstances, but we can change our attitudes toward God in them. In light of the promises of God, we can live "Giving thanks always for all things unto God..." Ephesians 5:20. He has not left us without hope!

The names and exact place of the following event escape me, but the lesson it taught me has never left my memory. A missionary family was flying over a large mountain range. The father was piloting the plane with his wife in the passenger's seat up front. Their two children were safely tucked behind their parents in separate seats. For some reason, the plane suddenly crashed into the top of one of the mountains. The parents barely escaped from the burning wreckage. Because of the intensity of the heat they were unable to rescue their children. They had no choice but to helplessly watch the flames consume their darling son and daughter trapped within. When a rescue team arrived, they were amazed to find the parents sitting together on top of that mountain, singing heartfelt praises to God. Together their countenance radiated a peace that was beyond mere human comprehension. We will not rejoice because of the circumstances, but we can rejoice in the promises of God, whatever may come our way. When God is real in our lives, we will learn to trust him as they did. Paul, a man who suffered many misunderstandings, persecutions, and heartaches, wrote Philippians 4:4, "Rejoice in the Lord alway: and again I say, Rejoice." and "In every thing give thanks: for this is the will of God in Christ Jesus concerning you. I Thessalonians 5:18

In conclusion

The Lord is looking for those who will love him, seek his will, worship him, and gladly obey him. The first three verses of Psalm 119 say, "Blessed are the undefiled in the way, who walk in the law of the LORD. Blessed are they that keep his testimonies, and that seek him with the whole heart. They also do no iniquity: they walk in his ways."

Looking again at King David's words, we see his wonderful example of devotion to God. "As the hart panteth after the water brooks, so panteth my soul after thee, O God. My soul thirsteth for God, for the living God…" Psalm 42:1, 2. David loved the Lord and wanted to please him. Nevertheless, he realized that he had the tendency to wander. Knowing this he asked the Lord to help him. "With my whole heart have I sought thee: O let me not wander from thy commandments." Psalm 119:10. In another passage we see his heart's cry, "Search me, O God, and know my heart: try me, and know my thoughts: And see if there be any wicked way in me, and lead me in the way everlasting." Proverbs 4:23; Psalm 139:23, 24.

Like David, if our hearts are going to abide in a right relationship with the Lord, we will have to be aware of our weaknesses. According to the word of God, what a person does stems from the heart of the individual. That is why we are exhorted to "Keep thy heart with all diligence; for out of it are the issues of life." Proverbs 4:23. Cultivating a tender heart toward the things of God is essential in order for us to recognize the sins and weights which hinder our lives. Then, we need to make changes as the Lord reveals those things to our hearts (see Hebrews 12:1). It is clearly our responsibility to make good judgments and take the steps necessary to purge our lives of anything that keeps us from being the examples we should. "If a man therefore purge himself from these, he shall be a vessel unto honour, sanctified, and meet for the master's use, and prepared unto every good work." II Timothy 2:21.

Job was another prime example of loyalty to God. We can perceive his heart through his prayers. "That which I see not teach thou me: if I have done iniquity, I will do no more." It is no wonder that the Lord God spoke so highly of this man! "And the LORD said unto Satan, Hast thou considered my servant Job, that there is none like him in the earth, a perfect and an upright man, one that feareth God, and escheweth evil?" Job 34:32; 1:8. Could the Lord use you as an example of one who desires to honor and please him in all you do?

These men were not super humans who somehow deserved a relationship with God. They were just like the rest of us. They had times of victory, failure, laughter, weeping when they felt pain; but they walked by faith. The Lord speaks to man, woman, boy, and girl — but only those who listen and respond will have victory. He calls us to a closer walk with him with such words as, "Come unto me, all ye that labour and are heavy laden, and I will give you rest. Take my yoke upon you, <u>and learn of me</u>; for I am meek and lowly in heart: and ye shall find rest unto your souls." This verse speaks of spiritual rest, not physical. "...And ye shall find <u>rest</u> <u>unto your souls.</u>" Are you tired and weary? Jesus said, "Come unto me." Matthew 11:28, 29.

The Lord said in Jeremiah 29:11-13, "For I know the thoughts that I think toward you, saith the LORD, thoughts of peace, and not of evil, to give you an expected end. Then shall ye call upon me, and ye shall go and pray unto me, and I will hearken unto you. And ye shall seek me, and find me, when ye shall search for me with all your heart."

Have you ever knocked on someone's door only to be disappointed when no one answered? Well, it will never be so with our Lord. He will readily answer all who seek his face, fellowship, and grace. "Ask, and it shall be given you; seek, and ye shall find; knock, and it shall be opened unto you: For every one that asketh receiveth; and he that seeketh findeth; and to him that knocketh it shall be opened." Matthew 7:7, 8. The Lord has promised to reward the diligent seeker, "...for he that cometh to God must believe that he is, and that <u>he is a rewarder of them that diligently seek him</u>." Hebrews 11:6.

Chapter 3

Surrendered to His Glory

That we should be to the praise of his glory, who first trusted in Christ. Ephesians 1:12

Have you ever heard someone say, "My purpose in life is to be a wife," or "My purpose is to be a mother," or "Miss Jones' purpose is to play the church piano?" Although these are all gifts and callings of God, none of them is a woman's primary purpose for living. What happens when the pianist develops arthritis and can no longer play, the wife becomes a widow, or the mother loses her children? Does she no longer have a purpose for living? On the contrary, she still has the same purpose she has always had – to bring glory to God. Any of these things can be done without bringing him glory in the process. This is just as true for men who are preachers, evangelists, teachers, working secular jobs, etc. The smallest task will either be done to God's glory, or it will not. If we live in light of our true purpose, we will endeavor to bring him glory in all things. As a result, our lives will be much richer, more fruitful, and valuable to others.

God's revealed glory

There are various ways in which God reveals his glory. For instance, He revealed his glory in Jesus Christ. "For God, who commanded the light to shine out of darkness, hath shined in our hearts, to give the light of the knowledge of the glory of God in the face of Jesus Christ." And Jesus, "Who being the brightness of his glory, and the express image of his person..." II Corinthians 4:6; Hebrews 1:3. (see I Timothy 3:16; Isaiah 9:6-7). There are numerous passages which proclaim that the glory of God is seen in Jesus Christ!

God's great glory is also displayed by the heavens above. How often has man gazed with awe at God's revealed glory? Even if a man or nation is without the written word, the heavens say to each heart, "There is a God"! "The heavens declare the glory of God; and the firmament sheweth his handywork. Day unto day uttereth speech, and night unto night sheweth knowledge. There is no speech nor language, where their voice is not heard." Psalm 19:1-3. "For the invisible things of him from the creation of the world are clearly seen, being understood by the things that are made, even his eternal power and Godhead; so that they are without excuse." Romans 1:20. Not one human being will be able to plead ignorance to the reality of Almighty God – the heavens leave them without excuse!

On a mission trip to Zambia, I had the privilege of seeing Victoria Falls before flying out of Livingstone. That evening, while on the Zambezi River, which feeds the falls, I had the opportunity of speaking to an African man concerning his need for Christ. (I usually have tracts with me but had left them in my tent. For him to receive the gospel, I was going to have to speak to him personally.) After sharing the gospel with him for a good while, I wrote several verses down for him to look up later. After he expressed his humble gratitude and went below deck, I noticed the sun was lowering quickly, and that the pontoon boat we were on was heading for shore. Settling myself on the bench, I leaned over the rail and looked toward the western sky. My breath momentarily stopped as my eyes beheld one of the most stunning sunsets I had ever seen. The extraordinarily beautiful mixture of reds, gold, grays, and blues against the blackening sky was enough to call the attention of every eye below. The beautiful colors on that African evening were vividly magnified by the sunlight which gave them their brilliance. I found myself wishing the sun would lower less quickly. Down, down it went—so swiftly, that it seemed to me I could actually see it moving. Though the breathtaking scene continuously changed, it never lost one moment of its glory.

I wanted to somehow capture the scene but knew it was not possible. No man or film could ever duplicate such magnificence to its fullest! My photos are only replicas – gorgeous scenery, but not nearly as splendid as the heavens I beheld. Never again would I see that exact same display of God's glory, but I would see others. His word says, "Night unto night uttereth knowledge." As long as there are nights and days, there will be a continuously changing exhibit in the heavens declaring God's infinite glory. If that which he has created is able to make such a glorious impression on our souls, what will that moment be like when we behold our Saviour in the fullness of his glory? "Looking for that blessed hope, and the glorious appearing of the great God and our Saviour Jesus Christ." Titus 2:13. How could anyone deny there is a God? Oh, yes, the heavens declare that he is, and that he is glorious!

Thy glorious grace!

We should continually thank the Lord for saving our unworthy souls by his "glorious grace"! (see Ephesians 1:6, 12). Because of his grace, we also have the power to walk in newness of life. Throughout the scriptures we are urged to "...walk worthy of God, who hath called you unto his kingdom and glory." Also, without the grace of God we would not understand how important it is to deny ungodliness (Titus 2:11, 12).

God's grace enables us to live in light of his purpose. "... all things were created by him, and for him." Colossians 1:16. "And we know that all things work together for good to them that love God, to them who are the called according to his purpose." Romans 8:28. We need his grace because sometimes the "all things" are not so easy or pleasant. The Lord is not holding his grace back from us. He freely bestows it upon all who will receive. "And God is able to make all grace abound toward you; that ye, always having all sufficiency in all things, may abound to every good work." II Corinthians 9:8.

To walk worthy of the Lord, we must allow him to fill us with his Spirit, which simply means yielding ourselves unreservedly to him, so that he may reign in and through us. John said, "He must increase, but I must decrease." For more of Christ to be seen in us, it will require denial of self on our part. Self-will, Selfishness, Self-reliance, Self-exaltation, all of these destructive sins hinder our fruitfulness and conceal the glory of God in our lives. Jesus said, "Abide in me, and I in you. As the branch cannot bear fruit of itself, except it abide in the vine; no more can ye, except ye abide in me. I am the vine, ye are the branches: He that abideth in me, and I in him, the same bringeth forth much fruit: for <u>without me ye can do nothing</u>…Herein is my Father glorified, that ye bear much fruit…" John 15:4, 5, 8. The focus in this passage is not only that we bear fruit, but that the Father is glorified by the fruit we bear. We will not yield fruit to our fullest potential unless we allow Christ to have control.

Without realizing it, we are oftentimes extremely self-willed. Paul wrote that one of the prerequisites for choosing a bishop was that he not be self-willed (Titus 1:7). Ladies, it is just as important that we dethrone SELF if we are going to live for Christ. A Christ-centered life will manifest to others that God is, and that he has a will for all mankind. "And be not conformed to this world: but be ye transformed by the renewing of your mind, <u>that ye may prove what is that good, and acceptable, and perfect, will of God</u>." Romans 12:2. Can you imagine the difference that would be made in our homes, churches, communities, country, and throughout the world if each of us lived every moment with the glory of God in mind?

Jesus referred to the relationship he had with his Father, and directly related it to pleasing him. "…the Father hath not left me alone; for I do always those things that please him." John 8:29. Our heavenly Father offers his grace to us 24 hours a day, 7 days a week. He bids us to "come boldly unto the throne of grace, that we may obtain mercy, and find grace to help in time of need." Hebrews 4:16. The choice is ours. When faced with decisions throughout the course of a day, we need to choose that which will honour the Lord. If we draw from him that which we need, we will find that those circumstances and temptations which threaten to hinder us from living up to his glory are not more powerful than his grace.

Sure ways in which to glorify the Lord

By no means can we fully elaborate on every way possible to give God glory, but hopefully these few scriptural truths will help to provoke your desire and eagerness to do so.

* Firstly, our faith in God for salvation brings him great glory. Speaking of Abraham, Paul said, "He staggered not at the promise of God through unbelief; but was strong in faith, giving glory to God." (Romans 4:20). When our faith is in the promise of God for salvation, we are proclaiming to the world, "...that a man is not justified by the works of the law, but by the faith of Jesus Christ,...not by the works of the law: for by the works of the law shall no flesh be justified." Galatians 2:16. God is exalted when our faith is firm in the finished work of his Son for our salvation.

* Secondly, a living, active faith is necessary to see the glory of God. Speaking to Martha after the death of her brother Lazarus, "Jesus saith unto her, Said I not unto thee, that, if thou wouldest believe, thou shouldest see the glory of God?" John 11:40. The Lord is worthy of our trust. If he had ever failed us we would have a justifiable reason to doubt him; but he has not, nor will he ever!

* Thirdly, unity among the brethren brings God glory. "Now the God of patience and consolation grant you to be likeminded one toward another according to Christ Jesus: That ye may with one mind and one mouth glorify God, even the Father of our Lord Jesus Christ. Wherefore receive ye one another, as Christ

also received us to the glory of God." Romans 15:5-7. When we are envious, jealous, contentious, backbiting, or full of condemnation toward our brethren, we are not glorifying our God. The Lord Jesus, as high and holy as he is, is not ashamed to call God's children brethren; yet, we will oftentimes speak of them (our brethren) with contempt in our voices. "Only by pride cometh contention: but with the well advised is wisdom." Proverbs 13:10. Instead of applying scriptural principles, which would benefit them, we often use our energies to speak evil of them to others. When we speak to someone other than the person who has erred, most often our intent is to magnify ourselves as righteous, rather than help the offender. If we have ill-will in our hearts, we will most likely corrupt those to whom we are speaking with our sinful attitudes. The heart of a person is lifted up in pride that is quick to talk about the failures and sins of another; instead of going to that person personally as the scriptures instruct. God has an order as noted in Matthew 18:15-17. We are instructed to go to them with a humble spirit, desiring to help the one who has sinned that they may be restored. "Brethren, if a man be overtaken in a fault, ye which are spiritual, restore such an one in the spirit of meekness; considering thyself, lest thou also be tempted." Galatians 6:1.

Until pride in our own hearts has been taken care of, we should refrain from going to a brother or sister in Christ. If we approach another using a condescending tone we may cause more harm than good. Our attitude and tone of voice are extremely important when speaking to another. If our spirit is not humble, meek, and helpful, our pride will most definitely displease the Lord as greatly as their fault—and probably more so! Regarding the importance of attitude, Paul reminded fathers not to provoke their children to anger and thereby discourage them (Ephesians 6:4). If a father can discourage his own child by having a wrong spirit, what makes us think we are innocent when we discourage our brethren with a condescending tone or provocative spirit? If our hearts are right with the Lord, we will *humbly* and earnestly encourage our brethren to live to his glory as well, because we love God and our brethren!

To God be the glory!

Herod found out the hard way how dangerous it is to accept the praise of man, rather than, exalt the God of all praise! "And upon a set day Herod, arrayed in royal apparel, sat upon his throne, and made an oration unto them. And the people gave a shout, saying, It is the voice of a god, and not of a man. <u>And immediately the angel of the Lord smote him, because he gave not God the glory</u>: and he was eaten of worms, and gave up the ghost." Acts 12:21-23. There was no second chance for Herod! Likewise, we must be careful not to allow others to exalt us above measure, nor should we exalt ourselves.

God has purposely chosen the foolish, weak, despised, and base things of the world "<u>That no flesh should glory in his presence</u>." I Corinthians 1:26-29. If we are going to glory, we should be careful to glory in God who equips and enables us to do his work! "But he that glorieth, let him glory in the Lord." Seeing the harm of God's people desiring their own glory, Paul wrote, "Let us not be desirous of <u>vain glory</u>, provoking one another, envying one another." II Corinthians 10:17; Galatians 5:26.

DEF. *Vain*: 1. Empty; worthless; having no substance, value or importance. Every man walketh in a vain show. (Psalm 39) 2. Fruitless; ineffectual. All attempts, all efforts were vain. Vain is the force of man. 3. Proud of petty things, or of trifling attainments; elated with a high opinion of one's own accomplishments, or with things more showy than valuable; conceited. 4. Empty; unreal. 5. Showy; ostentatious.

Exalting ourselves is vain and will profit us nothing in the end. The truth is, we have no basis on which to glory in ourselves. "For who maketh thee to differ from another? and what hast thou that thou didst not receive? now if thou didst receive it, why dost thou glory, as if thou hadst not received it?" Paul, realizing his own weakness, publicly proclaimed, "For though I would desire to glory, I shall not be a fool..." I Corinthians 4:7; II Corinthians 12:6.

In conclusion

Let my heart be sound in thy statutes; that I be not ashamed.
Psalm 119:80

Each of us has the responsibility of glorifying God in all we do. "Whether therefore ye eat, or drink, or whatsoever ye do, do all to the glory of God." I Corinthians 10:31. By God's continual supply of grace we can grow more and more pleasing to him in all of our ways. The magnitude of his glory will one day be realized and acknowledged by all; but it will be to our shame if we have not glorified him as we should with our lives. "And now, little children, abide in him; that, when he shall appear, we may have confidence, and not be ashamed before him at his coming." I John 2:28.

When the Lord touches your heart about an area of your life, regardless of how big or small it may seem, I encourage you to yield to his will and allow his grace to change you into the woman he created you to be – a woman who glorifies him in *all* of her ways.

Chapter 4

Body and Spirit—I am the Lord's

What? know ye not that your body is the temple of the Holy Ghost which is in you, which ye have of God, and ye are not your own? For ye are bought with a price: therefore glorify God in your body, and in your spirit, which are God's.
I Corinthians 6:19, 20

How would you feel if you bought a new home and the previous owner refused to relinquish the right of ownership? Would you remain silent while he continued doing whatever he pleased in it? I think not! I sincerely doubt that anyone would take this sort of audacity lightly! I would kindly yet sternly ask him to take his hands off of what now legally belonged to me. How about you?

Likewise, we have been purchased with a price which far exceeds any worldly exchange of money or goods—the precious blood of God's own dear Son. God through the Holy Spirit now resides in us, and we should relinquish control. The Lord has given each of us stewardship over our body and spirit, but they belong to God. How do you think the Lord looks at us when we do whatever we want with that which belongs to him? The Lord said, your body and spirit are no longer your own! They are his, to be used for his glory, not your purposes. Thus, we must relinquish right of ownership that we may glorify our Lord.

Listening and learning

Speak, LORD; for thy servant heareth. I Samuel 3:9, 10

Realizing the need for exercise, many mornings I utilized the walking track near the house where I was staying. One day there was an older couple just ahead of me. I increased my pace to catch up with them. Handing them a gospel tract entitled *Where Are You Going to Spend Eternity?* I mentioned the importance of knowing the answer to this question. Not long into the conversation, I realized they had already been saved. As we continued walking and speaking about the Lord, the wife sweetly said, "When the Lord speaks to us, we need to listen." After a short pause, she added, "Most people don't listen to him, you know." I faintly smiled at her, acknowledging the sad truth of what she had said. Talking with her, it was clear to me that she was very teachable. Though this lady could have been more modestly dressed, she was very meek in spirit. I believe with her attitude, if she heard biblical teaching concerning modesty she would quickly respond in obedience to the Lord.

Contrary to the thinking of some, not every one who dresses less modestly than they do is a whore. That may sound strong, but I have heard God's people spoken to like dogs from pulpits, yet I have never seen God condemning his children. He will deal with and chasten us severely, but the love of God is ever present. The Bible says, "Speaking the truth in love." Ephesians 4:15. Truth and righteousness will never change, yet the manner in which we deliver them will determine whether we are ministering the law which kills, or the Spirit that giveth life. There are some women who rebelliously resist the word of truth and they should, most definitely be personally rebuked; but, let us not speak to God's people like they are condemned. Those who are saved are no longer under condemnation! If it were not for the mercies of the Lord and the blood of Christ, we would all be consumed!

Remember, not everyone dressed immodestly is purposely opposing God. There are girls and ladies who truly want to honour the Lord but have never known a higher standard than that of their church. Others are confused by differing opinions of Biblical modesty. If you are hungering and thirsting for righteousness, God will not leave you without instruction. Every woman that has a submissive heart and love for God has the inner desire to please the Lord. What some ladies lack are godly examples and good Biblical teaching (II Timothy 2:21).

What is modesty?

The definition of "modest" covers both inward *attitude* and outward *action*. The words we speak, the tones we use, our body language, as well as the clothes we wear all fall under the scrutiny of modest behavior. (It is interesting to note that the same word translated into English as "modest" was also translated "good behavior" when referring to the qualifications of a bishop in I Timothy 2:9 and 3:2.) To be a modest woman means to be a woman of good behavior as well as dress. Our actions are simply the expressions of our hearts.

There are women who have attitudes far from proper for Christian ladies. Some may clothe themselves modestly, yet their hearts are full of rebellion or bitterness. They may be deceitful, full of guile, or given to pride! When meeting a woman such as this, it is essential that we do not mistakenly think that her outward modesty is wrong just because her attitude is. In other words, if a woman is modestly dressed and has a *holier than thou* attitude, her apparel is not what displeases the Lord, it is her prideful heart. When Jesus dealt with religious people who were tithing yet lacked judgment, mercy, and the love of God, he said, "...these ought ye to have done, and not to leave the other undone." Matthew 23:23. Jesus clarified that they should have tithed of their possessions yet rebuked them for lacking the right heart attitude. God is not pleased when we have a right action with a wrong attitude. Modesty in dress will never cause God to excuse an un-Christ like spirit within. To understand more about modesty, it will help to look at a good dictionary.

DEF. *Mod'est*, 1. Properly, restrained by a sense of propriety; hence, not forward or bold; not presumptuous or arrogant; not boastful; as a modest youth; a modest man. 2. Not bold or forward; The blushing beauties of a modest maid. 3. Not loose; not lewd. 4. Moderate; not excessive or extreme; not extravagant; as a modest request; modest joy; a modest computation. (Noah Webster's 1828)

There are many commendable attributes spoken of in God's word which when corporately combined make a woman modest, such as being meek, quiet, poor of spirit, and discreet. <u>Meek</u> is to be mild of temper; soft; gentle; not easily provoked or irritated; yielding; given to forbearance under injuries. It also means to be appropriately humble; submissive to the divine will; not proud, self-sufficient or refractory. <u>Quiet</u> means to be still; free from alarm or disturbance; as in a quiet life; peaceable; not turbulent; not giving offense; not exciting controversy, disorder or trouble; mild; meek; contented. <u>Poor in Spirit</u> is to have a humble opinion of ourselves; to be sensible that we are sinners, and have no righteousness of our own; to be willing to be where God places us, to bear what he lays on us, to go where he bids us, and to die when he commands; to be willing to be in his hands, and to feel that we deserve no favour from him. It is opposed to pride, vanity, or ambition. <u>Discreet</u> means to be prudent; wise in avoiding errors or evil, and in selecting the best means to accomplish a purpose; circumspect; cautious; wary; not rash. It is the discreet man, not the witty, nor the learned, nor the brave, who guides the conversation, and gives measures to society. Pharaoh looked for a man to rule who was discreet and wise, and he found Joseph. (Genesis 41).

Before defining outward modesty, it is good to first understand what it is not. The following true account was shared with me by Mrs. Lee Marshall, who has been an evangelist's wife for many years, is a mother of ten, and grandmother of thirty four. While teaching ladies in jail, she asked, "What is modesty?" One woman firmly answered, "It means to be *dowdy!*" (meaning, awkward, ill-dressed, or drab). Another woman spoke up and said, "No, that can't be right. Mrs. Marshall is modest, but she isn't dowdy." The first woman thought she knew what modesty was but was incorrect. From the jail house to the church house there are other well-meaning ladies who define modesty incorrectly. To be modest does not mean that you have to wear old bags made of 1920's material and look like a prude. Equally important, modest does not mean unkempt or unclean. We are not *more* spiritual if our clothing is sloppy, dull, or if we choose only dark colors.

God called for fine linens made of gold, blue, purple as well as other beautiful colors to be used when making the tabernacle. Heaven will be full of colorful precious stones with a street of gold. The virtuous woman in Proverbs 31 "… maketh herself coverings of tapestry; her clothing is silk and purple." "The king's daughter is all glorious within: her clothing is of wrought gold." Psalm 45:13. The quality or price of a fabric has nothing to do with whether you are modest or not. Beautiful colors and materials are not sinful or displeasing to God. What turns anything good into something sinful depends upon the way we obtain it, if it takes precedence over the Lord, and the purpose for which it is used. When our hearts and motives are godly, we will naturally begin to produce a modest outward appearance.

Shamefacedness

In like manner also, that women adorn themselves in modest apparel, with shamefacedness... I Timothy 2:9, 10

Although shamefacedness is in the Bible, few women understand its true meaning. Some people mistake an excessively withdrawn girl or lady as shamefaced, but that may not be the case. She may be unable to communicate normally with a man as a result of sexual or emotional abuse. It is not a display of biblical shamefacedness. It is a damaged spirit she has. (If you have been hurt in this manner, the Lord is *able* to heal the broken-hearted and make you completely whole.) God does not want your spirit dominated by the fear of man, nor does he intend for you to remain in this broken condition. As a woman learns more of her position and acceptance in Christ, she will be able to walk confidently with God and others in light of that relationship. The wholeness she possesses in the Lord Jesus will become a reality in her life.

Shamefaced is not the same as being ashamed, although it does have an indirect connection. As Christians, if our conduct is forthright and godly we have no reason to be *ashamed*. If our conduct has been unbecoming of a lady, we ought to feel the shame of our behavior. *Shame* is something properly felt when we are made aware of dishonoring the Lord.

Shamefaced is an attitude of the heart which means bashful, having a downcast look; very modest. The inner beauty of a woman who is truly shamefaced is an absolute delight to behold! If we believed this truth, we would allow the Lord to further help us become more like Christ in spirit. Personally, I was void of any type of godly teaching or influence throughout my childhood. Being raised by numerous people other than my parents, I endured many hardships and became bold, brazen, and forceful in my spirit. After I graduated, I began working in the world, which only increased my immodest behavior. Later, when the Lord saved me at the age of twenty-six, I knew in my heart that I was far from being a godly woman. Though I had no idea of what it meant to be godly, the cry of my heart was "Lord, please make me a godly woman." I thank God that he has brought me so very far from the shameless woman I once was. It did not happen overnight. Even today, I am continually seeking the Lord to more thoroughly understand, experientially, the true definition of shamefacedness.

God created the woman to be a man's opposite. Men were created to be tough, brave, bold, and aggressive; while women were made to be soft, gentle, and reserved. This does not make a woman helpless! The virtuous woman "strengtheneth her arms." She is not a prissy, helpless woman who is afraid of breaking a fingernail. In our day, women are becoming more and more bold-faced, aggressive, and domineering. They are leading in the work place, leading in the churches, and leading in the home while the men are cooking their own dinners, cleaning the house, and making sure that they do not ruffle their wives' feathers. Boy, have we come a long way – down! Women today are rarely embarrassed by brash language or off-colored statements made by others. More shocking is the number of women who themselves speak in an off-colored fashion. As daughters of the King, we need to ask the Lord to help us become more sensitive to and aware of how shameful immodesty is, inwardly or outwardly. A shamefaced woman is one who is not bold-faced. She is not inclined to speak rashly. Instead of catching the eye of a man, she is more apt to avoid looking boldly into his face. She is quiet, meek, and reserved. The definition simply means the idea of downcast eyes or bashfulness. O the beauty and value of a woman who is truly shamefaced! (I Peter 3:4).

The purpose for clothing

Adam and Eve walked with the Lord in the Garden of Eden and enjoyed the blessing of a clean conscience—that is, until they sinned against him. The moment Adam sinned, their eyes were opened and they felt the intense shame of their nakedness. Trying to hide their shame, they made themselves aprons of fig leaves to wear. The coverings they produced were inadequate. After pronouncing judgment upon them, the Lord provided Eve and her husband with a covering acceptable to Him. Genesis 3:7, 21. "Unto Adam also and to his wife did the LORD God make coats of skins, and clothed them." We know the spiritual application here reveals the redemptive work of Christ to cover our sins. Nevertheless, in the physical realm the Lord made "coats" to *cover* their bodies! It is interesting that God still clothed their nakedness, even though they were the only two people on earth. The same word used for coats here is used elsewhere in scripture to refer to the outer garment of the high priest of Israel. This garment covered the entire length of his body. We will look a little further into the significance of this later.

A coat in our society is known as a heavier, *extra* outer layer rather than an initial covering against the skin, as Adam and Eve wore. Proverbs 31 also gives us another look at the purpose of clothing in the life of a virtuous woman. "She maketh herself *coverings* of tapestry; her clothing is silk and purple." The fabric and color are indicated here, but the *purpose* for her garments was to *cover*. It is beneficial to understand that God's primary *purpose* for clothing is to cover our bodies, not the adornment of them.

It is not sinful to wear beautiful colors or fabrics, unless it is our intention to purposely draw attention to ourselves. Traveling through Florida, I saw this sign over a clothing shop: FLIRT, Wear Your Clothes Do the Talking. Even the world knows that the choice of clothing a woman wears sends a message to those around her. According to Katherine Hamnett, a top British fashion designer, *Clothes create a wordless means of communication that we all understand.* Fashion is a language which tells a story about the person who wears it. What does your clothing say about you? There are beautiful colors, fabrics, styles, and designs of garments which are perfectly appropriate for a woman professing godliness, and there are others which are not. Do you choose clothing that sends the message of modesty to those around you?

If you are saved, the Spirit of Christ dwells within you, but that does not mean others *see* Christ in you. Peter taught that the hidden man of the heart should be our prominent feature. "Whose adorning let it not be that outward adorning of plaiting the hair, and of wearing of gold, or of putting on of apparel; But let it be the hidden man of the heart, in that which is not corruptible, even the ornament of a meek and quiet spirit...." I Peter 3:3, 4. If a woman by means of loud or costly adornment is drawing the eyes of others, it is not Christ she intends to magnify! God is neither dowdy, nor is he gaudy. *The woman who wears excessive jewelry, gaudy hairdos, clothes that are attention getters to show off riches, or that draw attention to the secret parts, is not a modest woman.* (Reflections of Feminine Modesty) Seeking *vain* glory is foolish and unprofitable. It may get us a little attention now, but in heaven we will find it was vain and unprofitable. When we dress for the day, our first priority should be to cover our bodies modestly, neatly, and in a fashion that will compliment our Lord and Saviour.

"Whatsoever ye do, do all to the glory of God." I Corinthians 10:31. Keep in mind that we are representatives of Christ. Ladies are most becoming when they possess a meek, quiet, and humble spirit (I Peter 3:4). A woman with this spirit depicts calmness, gentleness, submissiveness; she is unpretentious and humble in spirit. A woman does not portray these wonderful attributes when she is loud, pretentious, and attracting attention from others. Modesty truly is a matter of the heart, which will make an obvious difference in our total manner of life!

Modest – to be or not to be?

Like Isaiah, the more we see the Lord as he really is, the more we will perceive our attitudes and actions in light of God's divine attributes. When Isaiah saw the Lord high and lifted up, it not only changed his perspective of God but also that of himself. His heart was smitten with the reality of his own sinfulness as well as his nation's. Being humbled, he confessed, "Woe is me! for I am undone; because I am a man of unclean lips, and I dwell in the midst of a people of unclean lips: for mine eyes have seen the King, the LORD of hosts." Isaiah 6:1-5. As we perceive God's holiness to a greater degree, the way we view our sin will change significantly. Only then, will we repent and seek God's grace to change us for the betterment of ourselves, and others.

The Lord warned us to *consider our ways* (Haggai 1:7). He proclaimed "…my people doth not consider." (Isaiah 1:3). God is displeased when we are careless in how we represent him. Living a modest life does not happen without endeavoring to do so. We must purpose in our hearts that we are going to seek his will, serve him with determination, and obey him without reservation. Joshua said, "…Choose you this day whom ye will serve." Barnabas, when he came to Antioch "…exhorted them all, that with purpose of heart they would cleave unto the Lord." Joshua 24:15; Acts 11:23. When you dress, do you consider your choices and correct them if they are not pleasing to the Lord? Who are we exalting, ourselves or the Lord?

A wise woman is aware that the tempter will use any avenue he can to distract her focus from the Lord. Satan will also use a woman's lack of modesty to distract the focus of others. If we are not thoughtful in choosing our attire, we can allure the eyes of men and encourage other girls and ladies to seek after the vanities of life. With the Lord's help, a godly woman will be careful of her conduct and dress so as not to influence others wrongly. There are times when even the godliest of women fall prey to Satan's devices. A little flirtatious look at a man, a certain gesture, a flattering tongue, or provocative dress; as small as these may *seem*, they are a great stumbling block to men. Ladies, it is our high calling to display the holiness of our Lord and Saviour Jesus Christ. If we fail to consider the righteous kingdom to which we belong, our perception of God's holiness will be clouded, and discernment between right and wrong will be lacking. If we are looking unto Jesus, we will not be led astray easily. Rather, we will lay aside the weights and sins that so easily beset us, and shine more and more brightly as we wait for the soon return of Christ (Hebrews 12:1). What may seem to be simple little choices each day make a big difference as to the extent that God is glorified in and through our lives.

The acceptable rule of measure

...but they measuring themselves by themselves, and comparing themselves among themselves, are not wise.
II Corinthians 10:12

No one can determine by human reasoning, or trust his feelings to correctly conclude what nakedness is or what is meant by being properly clothed. The biggest mistake women make in our day is to rely on what feels right, or to look at others for their standard of modesty or conduct. Comparing ourselves one with another is to err grievously. "For we dare not make ourselves of the number, or compare ourselves with some that commend themselves: but they measuring themselves by themselves, and comparing themselves among themselves, are not wise." II Corinthians 10:12.

We were designed by the Lord Jesus Christ to magnify his wisdom, righteousness, and holiness. If convictions do not come from the word of God, <u>the wrong rule of measure is being used</u>. *There are folks in our day who think that you are not naked unless you are totally unclothed. But it is possible to be partially naked, and without God's definition you will not know when you are or are not displaying nakedness.* (Davis, The Language of the Christian's Clothing) God's word is the accurate means of measure.

It is crucial that we remember that God will not compromise his holiness for you, me, or anyone else. He redeemed us unto himself and ordained that we should be holy. "For I am the LORD your God: ye shall therefore sanctify yourselves, and ye shall be holy; for I am holy..." Leviticus 11:44. Paul exhorted Christians in Romans 12:2, "And be not conformed to this world: but be ye transformed by the renewing of your mind, <u>that ye may prove what is that good, and acceptable, and perfect, will of God</u>." We are to manifest to the world that God has a will for our lives. The holiness of God is the only proper rule of measure. If the world is going to realize by our influence that God is Holy, we must be holy!

No one is apt to accept a higher level of modesty than that which they consider necessary to please God. Therefore, if I regard myself, my church, or another individual as having reached an acceptable level of modesty, I could easily *feel* that I am doing quite well according to my measuring stick. But, when I use the correct rule of measure and compare my level of modesty in light of God's holiness, I will perceive that I still have some growing to do. When the standard you or I have is other than the holiness of God, we have focused on a lesser standard and will never move closer to His. God's standard is assuredly much higher than ours. Remember, our purpose for living is to glorify the Lord, not to please ourselves. When we desire to honour our Saviour, we will be delighted to do whatever pleases him.

But that which ye have already hold fast till
I come. Jesus speaking to a church - Revelation 2:25

Have you ever been in a boat and turned the motor off to fish or relax awhile in a peaceful spot? Do you remember how calm it was as you laid back to watch the clouds roll by, and all of a sudden you realized that you had drifted far from where you once were? You were shocked to find how far downstream you had drifted. Likewise, once the Lord has taught us wonderful truths pertaining to godliness, we must be careful to diligently hold to those truths. What an awful feeling it is when we realize that our hearts have drifted far from God. Thank God for the sweet Holy Spirit who is faithful to point out areas in which we are slipping. Not only must we guard ourselves from carelessly drifting away, we should diligently continue moving upstream. There is no place to drop anchor in respect to Christian growth!

The responsibility of representation

Traveling overseas, I have noticed that in some countries their women are culturally more modest in dress than the majority of American women. One reason for this is that they have not yet been greatly influenced by the materialism and vanity of the Western world. Walking among them, I can say without hesitation, they knew at a glance that I was from another place! My features, skin color, as well as customs were clearly unlike theirs.

For instance, while I was helping a missionary family in Busan, South Korea, there was an American military base located on the opposite side of this large city of four million souls. During my stay, I saw only one other American on our side of town (a civilian - probably there to teach English in one of their schools). I would sometimes see this man at a bus stop near where we stayed. Although happy to see someone from home, there was something about him that disturbed me. I had not witnessed him doing anything obnoxious or illegal. What troubled me was his appearance. He had long scraggly hair and an earring in one ear. He sometimes wore a bandanna rolled up and tied around his forehead, his pants and shirt looked three sizes too big, and a hot iron sure would have helped. Whether he realized it or not, to the Korean people he represented all Americans. I had nothing against him personally; nevertheless, every time I saw him I felt a twinge of disappointment for his careless representation of the American people. This man was probably oblivious of the effect he was having on our reputation. Nevertheless, his ignorance did not make his poor representation any less distasteful. Likewise, if we do not carefully consider the importance of our conduct in this world, we will leave erroneous and negative impressions in people's minds concerning Christ and his kingdom.

In conclusion

Give unto the LORD the glory due unto his name; worship the LORD in the beauty of holiness. Psalm 29:2

During our short journey through this life, we represent God to the lost, as well as to our weaker brethren. The responsibility of being good examples has been given to us, whether we acknowledge that responsibility or not! It is up to each of us *what kind* of example we will be. The world should be able to perceive by our meek and quiet spirits and modest appearance that we are not as they are. We are ambassadors of another country – a heavenly country – one that is filled with God's holiness, righteousness, and glory! If we allow ourselves to be conformed to this world, its citizens will have no reason to think of us as strangers in their land. Also, our younger Christian brethren will have difficulty finding the way if our lights are not brightly shining to lead them. "Let your light so shine before men, that they may see your good works, and glorify your Father which is in heaven." Matthew 5:16. Like Jesus, are you willing to always do those things that please your Father? (John 8:29).

One of the men in my church made the following statement to parents, although the principle may be applied to any position of influence. "What you do in moderation your children will naturally do in excess." For their sakes, hold the standard of holiness as high as possible. Young minds seldom rise to the level of their mentors and examples. Each and every woman will be held accountable before God for how she influences those around her. I would like to make an even stronger appeal to ladies who are expected to have knowledge of God. James, writing to the brethren, reminded those who are in a place of influence, "We shall receive the greater condemnation." You and I are going to be held accountable for the way we influence every heart that is looking to us as an example. As a grandmother, mother, Sunday school teacher, pastor's wife, or any other area of influence, you are either provoking ladies to live godly, modest lives, or you are a stumbling block. Young or unlearned Christians around you do not know enough about God to understand the importance of modesty. Until they learn differently, it is you that they will look to as an example. Your attitude, conduct, and every article of clothing you wear will speak volumes. We are epistles known and read of all men (II Corinthians 3:2). Others should surely know by your conduct that you desire to grow, honor God, and worship the Lord in the beauty of holiness. When they know in their hearts that you are daily seeking to personally grow more pleasing to the Lord, they will be encouraged to do likewise.

Chapter 5

The Value of a Modest Woman

*Whose adorning let it not be that outward
adorning of plaiting the hair, and of wearing of gold,
or of putting on of apparel; But let it be the hidden
man of the heart, in that which is not corruptible,
even the ornament of a meek and quiet spirit, which
is in the sight of God of great price.* I Peter 3:3, 4

The Lord referred to the hidden man as having great price (worth). We ladies buy little gadgets for our homes. Now and then, I find some little object that turns out to be worth its weight in gold. For instance, I have a little square rubber gripper that helps me open those unruly jars when no one else is around. It cost me little and has no beauty, but it is most valuable to me. When we buy that fancy, decorative item that we just adore; often, as soon as the newness wears off, that wonderful item is now doomed to be sold in our next yard sale for little or nothing. The things that are most valuable to us are not necessarily the pretty ones, but rather, the useful ones. In God's sight, it is of *great* worth for a woman to have a modest spirit. The virtuous woman has a worth far above rubies (Proverbs 31). I have seen women who by the world's standard have unattractive features, yet their spirits radiated a pure loveliness that is rarely seen in our day. A woman like this affects others around her to the glory of God. On the other hand, I have seen women who had natural, outer beauty, yet their spirits were domineering, loud, pretentious, and disgraceful.

Instead of becoming a woman of great worth in the sight of God, worldly minded women spend their time and money trying to become more outwardly attractive to mankind. Largely influenced by the world's misguided sense of values, they put

55

the emphasis on good looks, sexuality, and glamour. Psalm 1 speaks of the blessedness of the person who refuses *ungodly* counsel. "Blessed is the man that walketh not in the counsel of the ungodly, nor standeth in the way of sinners, nor sitteth in the seat of the scornful." Before we will resist the counsel of the ungodly, we must recognize it for what it is. Women lower their worth when they follow after the vanities of this world. A wise woman will seek and follow the counsel of godly influences and God's word. "...But his delight is in the law of the LORD; and in his law doth he meditate day and night. And he shall be like a tree planted by the rivers of water, that bringeth forth his fruit in his season; his leaf also shall not wither; and whatsoever he doeth shall prosper." When we consider our apparel for the day, we should start by putting on the new man which is created in righteousness and true holiness (Ephesians 4:24). God will bless you for it.

A Clear Distinction

Men and women were obviously created with different physical characteristics, but there are inward differences as well—such as the way we think, feel, and the way we are affected by outside influences. More particularly, the passions of a man are much stronger than a woman's. While a woman is stimulated by touch, a man is stimulated by sight. As women, we will never understand *experientially* how a man feels or the extent he struggles in the area of lust. Why? Because we are not men. We simply do not think or feel as a man does!

Society is full of ungodly women who knowingly and cunningly use their bodies and clothing (tight, skimpy, or flashy) to attract the interest of men. These women are deliberately provoking men to lustful actions. The destructive effects that nakedness is having in our society are not difficult to see. As necklines have lowered and hemlines raised, so the number of rapes, incest, and other sex-related crimes has increased. Then there are women who are unaware of how forcefully their immodest apparel stimulates fiery passions within the opposite sex. An immodestly dressed woman may think a man is simply admiring her — and she likes to be admired — but often there is much more going on within him. Because a man's passions are triggered more easily, the sight of a woman's nakedness or the curves of her body have a seductive affect on his heart and flesh. A good comparison was made in *Reflections of Feminine Modesty* that will help explain this truth. *If a nice-looking man was constantly coming up to you and stroking your arms or your neck or your shoulders and gently touching you, how would that affect you? Sensually! That is the same effect a woman has on a man when he sees her wearing a short skirt; a tight, low cut, see-through, or sleeveless blouse; or a pair of pants.* Though a woman may not realize the degree that her immodest dress affects men, she certainly knows that her behavior attracts a great interest, and she knows furthermore that it is a sexual interest.

The shape of a woman's breasts, buttocks, or legs was never intended to be seen by any man other than her own husband. When an unregenerate man sees a woman immodestly dressed he can have wicked, vile, and disgraceful thoughts. No one may know his imaginations except him and God. Then there are godly men who strive to keep their hearts pure. They are not given to wickedness, but their flesh is weak! Because of their flesh, they are still capable of entertaining wicked thoughts when tempted. Ladies, if you are dressed immodestly or have a seductive spirit, a godly man will, at best, have to struggle to guard his mind and heart in your presence. The following true story helped me understand this truth: While visiting a couple in their home, the visitor noticed that the husband, who is a godly gentleman, showed signs of being uncomfortable in her presence. She noticed that he had glanced at her and then quickly turned away. She inconspicuously looked at herself, wondering what had triggered this reaction in him. She felt very uncomfortable when she realized that even though her skirt was long and loose and her neckline plenty high, her top was too tight. Until then, she had not realized how her breasts emphasized drew attention. Because she loves the Lord, she was deeply ashamed when she realized the affect her carelessness had on this man. When a woman is dressed modestly, her attire will not cause a man to feel the need to guard himself in her presence. It grieved her heart that she had given occasion for this godly man to struggle.

Yes, there are some men who are given to perversion and will lust regardless of how modestly a lady is dressed. We are not responsible for the lusts of men when we are not helping to provoke those lusts. Yet, God *will* hold us responsible when we allow ourselves to be a stumbling block to men in general, and especially to our brothers in Christ. The following helpful thought is from a small booklet entitled *The Sin of Bathsheba*. It is a gracious yet strong plea for women to carefully consider their effect on the male gender: *Oh that you could understand the fierce and bitter conflict in the souls of your brethren when you provoke them by the careless display of your body. Oh that you could hear their pleading with God for help and deliverance from the power of those temptations. Oh that you could see their tears of shame and repentance when the temptation has overcome them, and they have sinned with eyes and heart and mind. Never again would you plead for your right to dress as you please...you have no right to destroy with your careless dress the brother for whom Christ died...you are duty bound to glorify God in your body – to clothe that body, not as you will, but as God wills. And real love for your brethren would remove forever from your heart the desire to dress as you please. For, "We that are strong ought to bear the infirmities (that is the weakness) of the weak and not to please ourselves. Let every one of us please his neighbour for his good to edification. For even Christ pleased not himself..." Can you not deny yourself a little comfort or bear a little reproach for being "old-fashioned" or "out of style," in order to help another in his battle against sin?* (Cloud, The Sin of Bathsheba)

58

In conclusion

A godly man respects a woman who does not excite feelings within him that he knows should not be entertained outside of marriage. It is a serious matter for any woman to dress in such a fashion that would give occasion for men to sin. Jesus taught that lust in the heart of a man is as vile as the act of adultery itself. "But I say unto you, That whosoever looketh on a woman to lust after her hath committed adultery with her already in his heart." He went on to say that "If thy right eye offend thee, pluck it out, and cast it from thee: for it is profitable for thee that one of thy members should perish, and not that thy whole body should be cast into hell." Matthew 5:28-29. Pluck out his eye rather than to look upon a woman to lust! How could anyone doubt the seriousness of what the Lord is saying? Each of us has the potential of helping our brothers honour God, or we can help the devil destroy them through subtle temptation! What we must ask ourselves is this, "Do I want to give occasion for my brother to sin against the Lord!" If not, then be careful to dress yourself modestly. When a woman cares more about being noticed than the well-being of others, she is desperately lacking the love of God in her heart (charity). Charity seeketh not her own. It vaunteth not itself (see I Corinthians 13:4-6). God has not given us liberty to dress any way we please. "For, brethren, ye have been called unto liberty; only use not liberty for an occasion to the flesh, but by love serve one another." Galatians 5:13. When we love the Lord as we should, our clothing will not be selected in order to attract attention. When we love mankind as God loves them, we will desire to have a godly influence on others. "Favour is deceitful, and beauty is vain: but a woman that feareth the LORD, she shall be praised." "...for her price is far above rubies." Proverbs 31:30, 10.

Chapter 6

Modesty in Practice

But be ye doers of the word, and not hearers only,
deceiving your own selves. James 1:22

This chapter contains examples of modest and immodest clothing for the benefit of all. Neither the author nor this booklet is the measuring stick, for one good reason: I am still growing in grace and the knowledge of the Lord. I would be foolish to think that I have no need of becoming more modest in light of the vast holiness of God. The purpose of this chapter is not to give you a law which will make you righteous and secure your entrance into heaven. Righteousness is received when one puts their faith in Christ alone for salvation. Once you have received Christ, having his righteousness should create within us a desire to walk in light of that righteousness. Good principles do not become effective unless they are put into practice. A woman after God's own heart will seek out godly principles for modesty and apply them to her life. Remember, we are not our own. We have been bought with the precious blood of Christ.

What would you think if someone told you that his pastor is just too caring, or the English teacher is too educated in grammar, or a mother is too concerned about her children? We would think such a statement was ridiculous. We rightly expect people to excel to the very highest level in whatever they do. Why would we think it strange when a lady desires to be modest? Is it possible for anyone to be *too* godly, or *too* holy, or *too* modest? (We have already discussed that when a modestly dressed woman thinks herself to be better than others, it is her attitude that is sinful, not her modest clothing.) In order to be *too* modest we would have to exceed the holiness of God. And that, of course, is not possible! We need more ladies who are willing to learn and receive truth about modesty, who with the Lord's guidance will apply godly principles to their lives. We all have plenty of room for growth in godliness, inwardly as well as outwardly. It recently occurred to me that even in heaven we will be covered in white robes of righteousness. I'm not sure why the Lord chose white robes to express the covering of righteousness. It may very well be that white depicts purity and robes depict completeness. Whatever the reason, we won't be half covered in heaven and we shouldn't be half covered down here.

Over the centuries, dress has always been a means of identification. God instructed the priests of Israel down to the smallest detail concerning what they were to wear. In our day, we know a lot about a person by the way they dress. A business man in a suit can look across the street at a group of gang members. Their attire and actions clearly communicate the message of who and what they are. The Lord did not refer to the woman when mentioning a harlot; he referred to her attire and heart. (Proverbs 7:10). By merely mentioning her clothing, we all know the kind of woman to which the Lord was referring. He added that she was subtle of heart. Our attire says much about us. What we wear does make a difference and reveals our hearts!

Have you ever heard someone mention I Samuel 16:7 to excuse immodest dress? "…for man looketh on the outward appearance, but the LORD looketh on the heart." Sadly, those who quote this passage have never looked at the context. Samuel thought Eliab must surely be the leader God would choose—because of his sturdy physique. "But the LORD said unto Samuel, Look not on his countenance, or on the height of his stature…" The Lord was not looking for a servant who appeared *physically* capable, but he chooses a servant who is *inwardly* capable. Samuel was not referring to his apparel! He was looking at Eliab's <u>countenance</u> and <u>height</u>. Both of these are physical traits which Eliab had nothing to do with. Our clothing, on the other hand, is something that we have the power to control. When it comes to the way we represent God, the word of God puts great emphasis on apparel.

Scripture presented in context clearly shows that our outward appearance is very important to God!

The word of God teaches that, "Love worketh no ill to his neighbour: therefore love is the fulfilling of the law." Romans 13:10. If a woman truly has the love of God in her heart, she will care how she affects others. A wise woman will prayerfully and carefully choose what she wears. "Wherefore be ye not unwise, but understanding what the will of the Lord is." Ephesians 5:17.

Herein, you will find good, practical advice that will help you guard your testimony. It will be up to you to let the Spirit of God confirm in your heart that these examples are in agreement with the mind and word of God. A woman who is pure, humble, meek, and quiet in spirit will desire to grow more pleasing to the Lord, become more valuable to mankind, and more accurately portray the holiness of her Lord and Saviour. May the Lord bless you as you seek his will in regard to modesty.

Dresses or skirts

There is more to clothing than simply covering the body. Scripture distinctly mentions that we are to wear *modest* apparel. "The word for apparel is *"katastole,"* which is a combination of two Greek words. The first part, *"kata"* is defined by using the following words: covered, down, every, (far more) exceeding. The second part of the word is *"stole"* and was translated in Mark 12:38 as "long clothing." Mark 16:5 as "long white garment." In Luke 15:22, it is translated "robe," Luke 20:46 as "long robes," Revelation 6:11 as "white robes," Revelation 7:9 it is "white robes." In Revelation 7:13 it is translated "white Robes." In Revelation 7:14, it is translated "robes: 'They have washed their robes.' The word is consistent. When it says a long robe, that is exactly what it is referring to." (Davis, S.M.) It is clear that the definition of apparel is *exceedingly* clothed, yet the Lord still chose to connect the adjective MODEST, for further emphasis. Therefore, it is not difficult to conclude that if it is not long and loose (that is, not clinging to the body) according to the word of God it is not modest apparel. Dresses and skirts should be long and flowing.

What is a good length? Some believe that the garment must cover the thigh to be acceptable. Then, there are ladies who wear their dresses to mid-calf, and yet others near the ankle. We can look at whomever we choose for a guideline, but we would be wise to continue looking unto Jesus and his word. After the Lord Jesus Christ was resurrected, he appeared to John on the Isle of Patmos. The scriptures specifically mentioned that the garment Jesus was wearing covered him <u>to the foot</u>. "And in the midst of the seven candlesticks one like unto the Son of man, clothed with a garment down to the foot, and girt about the paps with a golden girdle." Revelation 1:13. Our Lord is clothed to the foot.

I offer you a thought provoking question. Would a woman be more modestly covered wearing a mini skirt or a dress reaching the top of her knees? Clearly it would be the longer one. All right, let us go a step further. Would she be more modest if her dress came further down to mid-calf? You understand the point. The more we cover our bodies, the more visibly modest we are. A woman who wears a dress that covers all of her legs would naturally be more modest than if her dress were just below her knees. If it is the holiness and righteousness of Christ we desire to display, can we be *too* modest? The extent to which a woman is or is not modest will not change the absolute holiness of God,

 but it will outwardly express her opinion of his holiness. If we are looking unto Jesus, we are looking in the right direction. If Jesus appeared to John wearing a garment down to his foot, I do not believe that we would be out of line to do the same. A friend of mine said, "If I'm going to err, I'd much rather err on the side of holiness." I agree, although I do not think we have to worry. No one is that holy yet.

Pants or slacks

Concerning attire, the Lord gave clear instruction to the sexes to remain distinct in dress one from another when he said, "The woman shall not wear that which pertaineth unto a man, neither shall a man put on a woman's garment: for all that do so are abomination unto the LORD thy God." Deuteronomy 22:5. *When God gave the distinctions between men and women in dress and hair length, He chose for the lady to wear a dress – a long, flowing garment – and hair that is long and flowing, which is more gracious and feminine and lovely than the appearance of a man. God directed for a man to wear pants or breeches and have a short haircut, which by nature is more masculine.* (What in the World Should I Wear?)

Pants have always been known as a declaration of authority. You may have heard someone say, "You can tell who wears the pants in that family." *Pants are a symbol of a man's authority, and when a woman wears them, she is displaying on her body a message about what's in her heart. (Davis, S. M.)*

Following are numerous quotes which clearly show that pants for women have only been accepted by American society since the 1900's. One article says: *It was not until well into the 1920's that anyone but the most indiscreet and daring women would wear trousers, even in the confines of her home. Initially, the new style was greeted with disapproval and ridicule.... The fad spread, wearing slacks to the office or to a park was still out of the question, and any female who appeared on a formal occasion in a trousers suit was assumed to be eccentric and probably [worse].* S. M. Davis further noted: *Years ago I was at the library doing research on the history of our church, and I came across an article from the Lincoln Courier from August 16, 1904.*

–An expected application from Postmaster McKay of Des Moines to be allowed to employ women as mail carriers and the fact that the regulations require these servants of the government to wear trousers have put the official of the postmaster in a quandary.

Sentiment in the department is strongly against allowing the use of women carriers, but careful search of the regulations reveals the fact that there is nothing there to prohibit them except they would have to wear men's apparel if employed. This section is plain and unmistakable in its intention to apply to men only, and refers without reserve to "pants, vest, and coat." A friend of the author, in Sauk Village, IL said, "Brother Davis, until 1957, it was against the law for a woman to wear slacks in the town of Sauk Village, IL." (Davis, S. M.)

A friend of mine, whose husband spent 20 years in the military, recently told me that she remembers when women were not allowed in the base commissary with rollers in their hair or wearing pants. How is it that what the world once looked upon as a shame is now acceptable to Christians? We know that our Lord does not change with the world, and neither should we! If something was an abomination to him last week, last year, or in ages past, is still an abomination to him today. Remember, the holiness of God is our rule of measure, not the world.

The following is an excellent example, revealing the focal point of a woman in pants: *A friend of mine told me that her decision to restrict her wardrobe to dresses and skirts came as a result of a ladies' class. All the arguments and reasons that could be given were unheeded until the lady who was speaking said, 'Let me just demonstrate something to you.' She asked the ladies in the audience to close their eyes momentarily. She held up a large picture of a woman in an attractive, feminine skirt and blouse. She asked the ladies to open their eyes. Then she inquired, 'What is the primary focal point to this picture? Where did your eyes first fall naturally?' The audience agreed that their eyes were first drawn to the face of the woman in the picture. She once again asked the ladies to close their eyes. When they opened their eyes they were looking at a large poster of a woman in a sport shirt and blue jeans. She asked, 'Now, be honest with yourselves, and tell me where your eyes first fell naturally when you looked at this picture?' Many of the ladies in the crowd were surprised to find that most people's eyes first focused upon [an area they all realized they should not be looking at] which was vividly emphasized before they ever noticed the woman's face. If this happened in a crowd of ladies, how much more would it be true of men? For my friend, this was all the 'evidence' that was needed.* (What in the World Should I Wear)

When I was saved in 1987, I knew nothing about godliness for a woman. At that time, I was working a man's job and wearing men's coveralls. In church, I heard the preacher say that the Lord does not want ladies wearing pants. I began praying about this new thing I had been hearing. One day, I stopped by the church to pick up a few gospel tracts to take to work with me. When I walked in, I saw several ladies cleaning the church wearing pants. I felt a bit confused, wondering why these ladies were not in dresses. After the preacher greeted me, I asked him, "Brother _____, why are these ladies wearing pants?" He looked grieved and said, "Sis, I preach that they shouldn't, but they say that they would be immodest bending or climbing in a dress." We will not debate this pastor's responsibility as the overseer of the church, but I will share with you my reaction. Even as a young Christian, that kind of reasoning did not make sense to me. In the early days of our country, women did everything they needed to in a dress. If it was loose enough they had plenty of room to move around freely. If it was long enough they did not have to worry about someone seeing up their dresses. Before cars were in existence, our ancestors rode in horse drawn buggies. When a lady stepped up into a wagon, she would graciously lift her skirt away from her foot and watch her step. Most women our day do not come close to working as hard as they did. We have been blessed with so many conveniences that most women would feel abused if they had to go without their washer or dryer for more than a week. They washed their clothes in a tub outside, milked the cow to make butter and cream, and so on, and they did everything in dresses that came to their ankles. The fact is, if a lady truly desires to glorify God, she is not going to make excuses to keep from doing so.

Blouses or tops

The fit of a blouse can be comfortably modest without looking sloppy. A good way to test for modesty is to examine yourself in the mirror. Be sure to look on the front as well as your profile. The length of the blouse should come down far enough below your waistline to keep your midriff from showing when bending over or raising your arms. We should also watch clingy materials, such as knit, spandex, and nylon. A garment that is too tight (such as some pullover sweaters or tops) will round under and draw attention to the breasts. It is worth taking the time to examine ourselves closely.

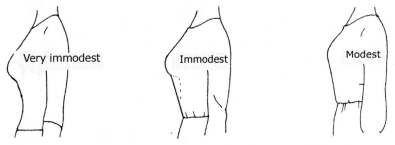

Very immodest | Immodest | Modest

<u>Bust line</u>: For a woman to be modestly covered, her dresses and blouses should be loose enough so the form of her bust does not draw attention. She should also make sure that the outline of the bra is not visible through the fabric.

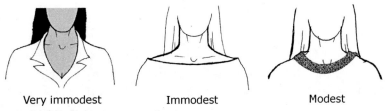

Very immodest | Immodest | Modest

<u>Neckline</u>: Some ladies use the "two finger rule." By laying two fingers crosswise starting at the front most part of your collar bone, you can trust the neckline to be safe. This measurement may vary slightly depending on your build. A neckline may be fine when you are standing upright yet become immodest the moment you bend over. The boat-neck style blouse has a wide

neckline and reveals more flesh. The closer the neckline is to the collar bone at the base of the neck, the more modest it is.

Here is something to consider. If you go to the altar to pray, remember that there are men in front of you on a higher elevation. A friend of mine, preparing to teach a ladies' class, asked the men of the church if they ever had to turn their heads while on the platform because of immodestly dressed women. Every man present said without hesitation, "Yes, on numerous occasions." Ladies, it is shameful that our men look down from the pulpit area not knowing what will be seen from their viewpoint.

Sleeveless: oftentimes, the armhole becomes a peek-a-boo hole, and more can be seen than a woman realizes. Many times a lady's undergarments will be showing. Also the tender, fleshy area of the bust and back near the underarm are sensual to most men. Therefore, they should not be worn.

Culottes

When God gave commandment to the priests of Israel concerning their attire, he instructed them to wear a linen garment called breeches. It is interesting that God cares so much about modesty that he had these men wear breeches under their linen coverings. "He shall put on the holy linen coat, and he shall have the linen breeches upon his flesh..." Leviticus 16:4. Because breeches covered his thighs, and because of the description in Exodus 28, some conclude that it must be proper to have the rest of the leg uncovered. Yet, if he had only his breeches on, he would be running around in his underwear! Breeches were worn under his robe, not apart from it. I feel much safer focusing on the priest's outer garment for a man's standard, rather than his undergarment. It is also interesting to note, that the priest's outer garment (worn over his breeches) hid the "form" of his buttocks. God is holy! Yes, I realize that men are dressing immodestly as well. There was a day when a man would have never walked in his own house, among his children, without a shirt. The only shorts a man wore was his undershorts, and no one other then his wife knew what color they were. But the modesty of men is not our focal point. We are looking at how we, as women, can improve in this area.

From a practical standpoint, culottes do not promote feminine characteristics. Most girls in culottes feel free to sit with their legs sprawled out or crossed like a man. Young ladies should be trained from their youth to act and sit like ladies everywhere,  especially in public. Some women who wear culottes choose a looser style saying, "If they are loose enough they look like a skirt." I agree that there are patterns that make some look like skirts – that is, as long as the girl wearing them is standing in one spot. The simple truth is, if you are walking and sitting like a lady, you do not need a crotch. If culottes look like a skirt, and you plan to conduct yourself like a godly young lady, then why not wear a skirt?

Even the world once put a high value on femininity and sometimes sent their daughters to finishing schools to teach them how to walk and talk like ladies. I'm not advocating that we send our girls away. Where would we send them anyway? The world no longer values what they once did. No, God has given us the responsibility of teaching our girls how to conduct themselves. Let us encourage them to become who God wants them to be—feminine, gracious young ladies.

Slits

It is sometimes difficult to find dresses or skirts that are not slit up the side or back, but it's not impossible. For with God nothing shall be impossible! No Christian should wear a skirt so tight that it needs to be cut in order to walk comfortably. The designers of such provocative attire know exactly what they are doing, and so do most women who wear them. The human eye is automatically drawn to anything that the mind recognizes as unnatural. If we ladies saw a man walking by us with his pant legs ripped up the side, it would draw our attention. A trigger would go off in our minds indicating that there is something around us that does not make sense. Slits are slits, regardless of how long or short the opening is. Because of the peek-a-boo affect, it draws attention to the leg. Most men find this very sensual, even more so than a shorter dress. Why compromise a little?

Slits can sometimes be fixed and keep you from having to use the garment for scrap material. If you have a skirt where the slit laps over, it can either be sewn together or iron-on seamstress tape used (just be sure it adheres well). There are other creative ways to fix a slit. You can have a seamstress attach a piece of cloth (not sheer) under the slit, or if you are able you can do it yourself. I am not a professional seamstress, but I have learned to sew out of necessity. If I have to take further lessons, I will do  so before I will be forced to accept the world's ungodly styles. Sewing is a very rewarding skill. If you already sew, you could be a blessing by teaching others this rewarding and useful skill. A modest woman is a godly example to others and will take the time and effort to be so.

Another important area often overlooked is that undergarments are not meant to be seen. A lady used to be ashamed if she walked out of the house and found that her slip was showing. More often, women's skirts or dresses have slits revealing part leg and part undergarment. I'm sure that they do not realize how sloppy this looks, or they wouldn't go out of the house that way. It may be better for men to see her slip rather than her leg, but it is very unbecoming. It reminds me of seeing a man with his underwear sticking out of the top of his britches. Ladies, if you'll make sure your undergarments are out of sight, you will be more modest as well as neat in appearance!

Sheer material

Another area worth mentioning is the sheerness of a material. For instance, thin cotton can be extremely revealing. This does not mean you cannot wear it. A heavier satin slip or high-necked camisole can be worn underneath, but one must take extreme caution when doing so. The undergarment should be modest enough that no one would ever know it were anything other than the natural lining of the outfit.

Often, a woman walking through the church doors with the sunlight behind her turns what should be a pure sight into an obscene view. If you have any doubt about the material of a garment, it is best to have a mother, sister, husband, or daughter look at you with the sun at your back. It is important to have good lighting. A garment may not be recognized as see-through until you are in the natural sunlight (this works for skirts as well). Women often walk into church, unaware that they are wearing a see-through blouse or skirt. I could have read some women's bra tags through their blouses.

If you live alone, find a window or open a door to let the sunlight in while you look in the mirror. If you have any doubt, it would be safer to find another outfit. It would be better to choose different garment than to find yourself embarrassed once you are out, and it is too late to change.

Hair, nails, and make-up

<u>Hair</u>: Most Christians lack a *biblical* understanding of the importance and purpose of a woman's hair. Most often, a woman will allow convenience and what makes her appear most attractive determine her style and cut, while forgetting that her hair is a God given symbol of submission (I Corinthians 11:2-15). After Eve sinned, God pronounced her judgment in Genesis 3:16, "...and thy desire shall be to thy husband, and he shall rule over thee." It is God's design that the man protects and guides the woman. It is her place to follow and rest in the Lord's guidance through her husband as she prays for him. As women in our society became more dominate there was a noted change in hair length. *One of the early warning signals of the women's movement was the bobbing of the hair. The "bob" was probably named after the boy's name Bob since the hairstyle is boyish. (Reflections of Feminine Modesty).* As women became less submissive, they also lost sight of their divine place of protection and the beauty of femininity. Like the church is to Christ, the woman is the glory of the man. "For a man indeed ought not to cover his head, forasmuch as he is the image and glory of God: but the woman is the glory of the man." I Corinthians 11:7.

Paul reminded the church at Cornith that a woman's hair was to have length. "Doth not even nature itself teach you, that, if a man have long hair, it is a shame unto him? But if a woman have long hair, it is a glory to her: for her hair is given her for a covering." I Corinthians 11:14, 15. The Greek word for "covering" in verse 15 is "peribolaion," which means: "something thrown around one, i.e. a mantle, veil—covering." This word is translated one other time in the New Testament as "vesture." "And as a vesture shalt thou fold them up..." Hebrews 1:12. Like this vesture (a garment that covers) a woman's hair is given for a covering.

How long is long? The word of God does not forbid ladies to trim their hair, nor does it refer to an exact length. Nevertheless, it does refer to *long* hair. "But if a woman have long hair, it is a glory to her: for her hair is given her for a covering." vs. 15. Longer hair represents an attitude of submission to authority and the femininity each of us should portray. (It is easy to see why it is a shame for a man to have long hair. The longer a man's hair the more feminine he looks.) A woman named Mary loved the Lord and used her hair to wipe his feet. "Seest thou this woman? ...she hath washed my feet with tears, and wiped them with the hairs of her head." (Luke 7:44; John 11:2). One thing is for sure, no one could have accused Mary of having short hair. Could we wipe the Saviour's feet with our hair?

In a letter to Timothy, Paul later dealt with another area of concern. He addressed the problem of ladies using their hair or apparel as attention getters. He instructed "...that women adorn themselves in modest apparel, with shamefacedness and sobriety; not with broided hair..." I Timothy 2:9. Peter dealt with adorning the hair when writing to the saints scattered throughout Asia Minor. "Whose adorning let it not be that outward adorning of plaiting the hair..." I Peter 3:3. I do not believe that it is a "sin" to put a simple braid in your hair any more than it is to wear apparel. The point is that we should not use braiding our hair as a means of attracting the attention of others.

Thus, we see two problems that were dealt with by two different men of God in two of the early churches. Some ladies were shortening their hair, while others were using their hair as a means of attraction. One last thought worth mentioning is this: since hair was given for a woman's covering, how can it be proper to pull it tightly back off of our ears and neck? A woman looks less feminine with her hair tightly pulled against her skull. When we take God's word seriously, we will take our covering seriously.

Hair Color and Nails: Society feeds on our natural desire for pleasure, beauty, entertainment, and education. None of these are bad things in themselves. They become a problem when we allow them to dominate our actions. Nearly everyone is trying to keep up with the Jones. Feeling inadequate, women are falling into the pit of pretentiousness. Genuine, down to earth people are so few in our society. Christians have forgotten that we have been fearfully and wonderfully made – just the way we are! (Psalm 139). We were made *by* the Lord and *for* him. Did he do it wrong? We should be clean, neat, and keep our vessels healthy and natural. Even society realizes the profit of "natural" things like shampoos, soaps, foods with no additives, naturally processed oils, all natural vitamins–there is no end. Yet, Christians are still obsessed by changing who they are naturally. Why would a woman be compelled to color her hair or nails a fake color? With so many diseases caused by chemicals, why would we willing expose ourselves to more potential harm? My hair is graying and the thought has crossed my mind to hide the fact that I am aging; but by the grace of God, I recognize my vanity and remember the beauty God has given me. The Lord said, "The hoary head is a crown of glory, if it be found in the way of righteousness." Proverbs 16:31. What are we following, the world's thinking, or God's?

Make-up: When you ask most Christians about make-up, you will rarely hear a biblical answer. Usually, carnal reasoning is used by those who have never sincerely prayed and sought God's will about the subject. It will help to reiterate the fact that *DO's* and *Do NOT's* are not the issue, but rather where is your heart in respect to God's will and glory? We need to consider *why* we make the choices we do – the *heart* of the matter so to speak. Our thinking is largely influenced by principles that we are introduced to and accept. Thus, it is important to examine the source of what we accept in order to see if it depicts spiritual or carnal thinking. Romans, chapter 8 reminds us that if we are going to please God, we must guard against being "carnally" minded. "For to be carnally minded is death; but to be spiritually minded is life and peace. Because the carnal mind is enmity against God: for it is not subject to the law of God, neither indeed can be." Romans 8:6-7. When we are carnally minded, we are agreeing with the enemies of God.

74

DEF. *Carnally:* In a carnal manner; according to the flesh; in a manner to gratify the flesh or sensual desire. (Noah Webster's 1828 Dictionary). So let us examine our thoughts and their roots. Why would any woman feel if she does not have dark eyelashes that she is not pretty, or if her lips are not glistening with color that she is not desirable? God's word does NOT promote these thoughts. They come from the world, not our Lord. When our thoughts do not agree with God's word, we are not "spiritually minded."

I am not saying if someone uses a cover-stick to hide a nasty blemish that they are ungodly; yet it does remind us that we are susceptible to vanity. A teenager who will not go out of the house because she has a zit, does not have a biblical perception of where her value really lies. According to God's word, our value to others is determined by the extent we allow Christ to reign in and through us, not our looks. Vanity focuses on self, not others.

Years ago, I experienced what happens when vanity controls our actions. As human beings, we all have been hurt by others. (There is always the initial pain we must deal with, but if we are going to be like Christ we must be willing to forgive.) After being cruelly treated by someone I greatly respected, I found myself in need of a friend to pray with. As I approached the house of someone I felt cared, I saw her curtains move and was relieved to find her home. I knocked several times but there was no answer. My heart sank further by her obvious indifference. Later, I asked her why she did not come to the door. Her reply was that she had not fixed herself up yet. I realized then the harmful effects of carnal thinking. Most of us would rather have a friend with messy hair or unwashed face, than ten who think more about how they look. For the record, many years have passed, and she and I are still friends. Like anyone yielded to the Lord, we are both growing as we recognize misguided priorities in our lives. With that said, let us simply look at what the word of God says about make-up. If you are allowing the Lord to minister to your heart, these passages and principles will help.

Make-up is mentioned twice in the Bible as having one's face painted. First, on Jezebel, a woman associated with fornication, seduction, and adultery. She was known as a manipulator of her husband, as well as other men. When Jezebel is mentioned in the New Testament, this is how God described her, "Jezebel, which calleth herself a prophetess, to teach and to seduce my servants..."

Jezebel was a seducer. "And when Jehu was come to Jezreel, Jezebel heard of it; and she painted her face...and looked out at a window." II Kings 9:30. It is interesting that the Bible notes that Jezebel painted her face before going to the window. Somehow, Jezebel's COVERGIRL only REVEALED her spirit of seduction. While looking into the definition of seduction, I noted Noah Webster's wise statement concerning the safeguard of principles: *A woman who is above flattery, is least liable to seduction; but the best safeguard is principle, the love and purity of holiness, the fear of God and reverence for His commandments.* It truly is a matter of the heart. A woman can safeguard herself by holding to godly principles. Likewise, godly principles will keep us from seducing the attention of others.

During my stay in South Korea, I saw the boldest form of seduction imaginable. One day I visited an area where there were numerous souvenir shops that attracted men from the US military base. While making my way through the crowded cobblestone streets, I was shocked to see one particular building with prostitutes advertising on every level. Each poised herself on a brick window ledge with her face painted and her intent unmistakable. They were seducing men to seek further fulfillment than a look could provide. No, not every woman who wears make-up is sitting in windows enticing men, but surely we can detect a bit of vanity behind the cover-up. What reason could a woman have for painting her face other than needing to feel accepted by others or to attract their attention? Is this spiritual thinking?

If a woman truly understands her acceptance in Christ and the completeness she has in him, she would not feel unattractive. Yes, we should radiate beauty; but the beauty that is most beneficial to man and pleasing to God is that which shines from within. Let's face it, if we were not bombarded by the sleek models of advertising that are craftily touched up by the graphic artists of the fashion world, we wouldn't be so tempted to paint our faces in order to feel pretty. If you compare yourself to that kind of a woman, you are sure to feel ugly because you are not as *glamorous* or as *alluring.* To "make-up" simply means to portray something other than it really is. With colors painted on her face or mascara coated eyelashes, a woman is not natural.

The second time "painted" is mentioned is when the Lord spoke of Israel, "For my people is foolish, they have not known me; they are sottish children, and they have none understanding: they are wise to do evil, but to do good they have no knowledge. Jeremiah 4:22. The Lord went on to say, "And when thou art spoiled, what wilt thou do? Though thou clothest thyself with crimson, though thou deckest thee with ornaments of gold, though thou rentest thy face with painting, in vain shalt thou make thyself fair..." vs. 30. "Favour is deceitful, and beauty is vain: but a woman that feareth the LORD, she shall be praised." Proverbs 31:30. If you make anything up, make up your mind that you are going to allow the Lord to renew your thinking. "That ye put off concerning the former conversation the old man, which is corrupt according to the deceitful lusts; And be renewed in the spirit of your mind; And that ye put on the new man, which after God is created in righteousness and true holiness." Ephesians 4:22-24 "Casting down imaginations, and every high thing that exalteth itself against the knowledge of God, and bringing into captivity every thought to the obedience of Christ." II Corinthians 10:5.

Worldly values will always bring us into bondage, but having the mind of Christ will give us liberty and peace in our hearts. It boils down to whether we believe the word of God or not!

"Vanity of vanities...all is vanity." Ecclesiastes 1:2. Will we give ourselves over to purity or to vanity? It is a choice we make each day. A woman who has her mind renewed by the word of God, thinks differently than the world. Ladies, let us determine to be real, unpretentious, and spiritually minded. Let the hidden man of your heart show the beauty and holiness that God, as well as your husband, will cherish. A good man knows when he has a good woman of great worth, and he will love her for her godly character!

The importance of gestures

As well as revealing apparel, we must remember that certain gestures can affect a man in a sensual fashion. For instance, in the process of stretching we can put our bodies in positions that are improper in the presence of men. The intention may simply be to loosen tight muscles, but while lifting her arms up and curving the spine forward, a woman is also throwing her chest and rear up and out. I am not suggesting that we never stretch, but I am bringing to mind that we should be careful not do so inappropriately. It can be very provocative! On another note, standing with hands on hips is not necessarily an immodest action, but this is a masculine posture that is unbecoming of a lady. Before the Lord saved me, I was an ironworker/welder and later became a pipefitter/welder. Working around all those men, I acquired many of their traits as I tried to fit in. The fact is, I did not fit in and should not have been trying. Oh, if only I would have had someone impart to me the wisdom I needed as a girl! If someone in my life would have known and taught me God's principles. My life would have been so different.

A little irritating factor we all face from time to time are those awkward moments when an undergarment just will not stay in place. Without realizing it, a lady may adjust an uncomfortable upper or lower undergarment in public. This is something that we need to catch ourselves before doing. When we can stand it no longer and must take care of that aggravating problem, it would be best to excuse ourselves quietly and escape to the ladies' room to do so.

Eye contact is also a powerful means of communication. The eyes of a person say much. They often say what the mouth does not. A flirtatious glance can cause a man to struggle inwardly. The word of God warns men to beware of a woman who attempts to attract with a flattering tongue or eyelids. "To keep thee from the evil woman, from the flattery of the tongue of a strange woman. Lust not after her beauty in thine heart; neither let her take thee with her eyelids. To take thee with her eyelids depicts force. For by means of a whorish woman a man is brought to a piece of bread: and the adulteress will hunt for the precious life." Proverbs 6:24-26. Ladies, it is perfectly all right for you to flirt with your husband (for the recorded, I strongly suggest that you do. He needs to feel that he is still your Knight in Shining Armor) but we should be careful how we look at and talk to other men. Flattery is deceitful, and a woman knows when she is using her tongue or eyes for advantage. It is an ungodly woman who uses a seductive tone or look to manipulate a man. Even if her words say nothing inappropriate, her tone and eyes say it for her.

As daughters of the King, we should portray the holiness and righteousness of our Saviour at all times. If we desire to glorify him, we will conduct ourselves properly in the presence of others.

Chapter 7

Helpful Hints

A wise man will hear, and will increase learning;
Proverbs 1:5

Let us not forget this wonderful truth: The effectual fervent prayer of a righteous man availeth much (James 5:16). As a young Christian, once I understood the importance of modest clothing, I was saddened to see the styles getting worse. Decent clothing was becoming harder to come by. Knowing that I was helpless to change the fashion trends of the world, I fell to my knees—not in despair, but in faith. I asked the Lord to change the designers' hearts to make skirts longer. Having the childlike faith of a young Christian, I was not surprised when I heard that the fashion world had taken an unexpected turn toward length. The Lord saved us to glorify him, and he is willing and able to supply our needs so that we can do so. I hear a lot of people complaining, but few mention praying. We have not because we ask not (James 4:2). The Lord promised, "And all things, whatsoever ye shall ask in prayer, believing, ye shall receive." Matthew 21:22.

Along with prayer, the Lord gave us good minds and principles, and he expects us to use them. I hope you will find helpful information in this chapter that will be an asset to your life.

Vests: I have found that a few nice vests are great to have around. The blouse underneath can be more snug than it should, but by adding a nice vest my form is covered, comfortably yet neatly.

Sleeveless jumpers: A blouse or shirt underneath a sleeveless jumper will assure you are modest. Cotton in the summer and a heavier material in the winter make a jumper a wonderful year-round garment. Lace to denim, you have many choices.

Be honest: Pride will cause a lady to buy a size 12 when she should purchase a 14. Trust me, she would look much better in a modest fit.

Robust women: Ladies with a larger bust size have to be more careful than those who are not so. It will be more difficult for you to keep your form neatly modest, though it is possible. It has a lot to do with the style and size you choose. Use wisdom.

Button up skirts: A friend shared with me that she adds additional buttons to the bottom of her button up skirt and then sews it together along the edge (from top to bottom). This gives the appearance that it was meant to button all the way down and keeps the buttons from slipping open. If you add additional buttons you don't necessarily have to sew it together, as long as they hold well. Lots of choices!

Taller women: Being on the taller side, I understand the difficulty in finding skirts or dresses that are conservatively long. There are a few articles of clothing in my wardrobe that come to my lower calf, which is not as long as I like. When wearing one of these garments in the summer, a petticoat with a soft, lace bottom always adds a feminine touch that looks and feels lovely, while adding length. (Sheets can be found at yard sales or thrift stores and make beautiful petticoats, inexpensively.) If you like more of a straight-line skirt, lightweight knee-high socks will come in handy. (You need to watch those straight cut skirts to make sure you will still be modest when bending or climbing stairs.) In the winter months, a pair of tights makes a nice contrast to an outfit, and they give added warmth in cooler climates. Boots, if they have low heels, are very practical and make a useful covering. I would make sure they are high enough so that your skirt remains over their tops once you sit down. This way you are not aggravated by your hem constantly catching on the top of your boots. You can be comfortably modest.

Swimwear: As God's children, we certainly should not wear the world's swim wear in public. If the pool is completely private, you are not sinning by swimming with your husband. The key word here is *private*. You and your husband's bodies belong to each other. It is when others can view parts of our bodies that only our husbands should see that we are immodest. Swimming with the family can be enjoyed when a little care is taken. I have a friend whose family swims in a creek near their home. Though with her family, a lady should never wear a T-shirt or any type of material that would cling to her figure once wet. I found that making a swim dress out of extremely lightweight, water-resistant material solved the problem, while fully covering me. I simply used a jumper pattern and added short, loose sleeves. Outside of the family, mixed bathing can subject you and your family to the immodesty of others if the highest principles are not upheld by all. Sadly, they usually are not.

Children's apparel: Ladies, if it is wrong for you, it is equally wrong for a 16 year-old or a small child to wear. It is best to start them out right and stay that way. You'll be glad you did. Telling a 12 year-old that the shorts she has been wearing since she was born are no longer proper, leaves her with the impression of double-mindedness. If you didn't learn the importance of modesty until late in your Christian life, by all means, it's better late than never. Be honest with your children about your past failures and prayerfully teach them God's principals from his word. Another thing to remember is that the number of perverts in our world is increasing daily, and they are interested in children! Do all you can to keep their bodies modestly covered, not only because it is right before God, but for their safety.

Men's attire: When the Lord used the word ABOMINATION to express how he feels about a woman wearing men's apparel, he left no room for doubt. "The woman shall not wear that which pertaineth unto a man, neither shall a man put on a woman's garment: for all that do so are abomination unto the LORD thy God." Deuteronomy 22:5.

82

Sometimes a lady who would not think to put on a pair pants will wear men's shoes to work outside. More often these days, we are seeing girls wearing men's ball caps. Some women carry men's wallets. A woman's attire is meant to be feminine and portray that she is the weaker vessel who should be cared for. The Lord does not want us in our men's shirts, socks, shoes, hats, or any other thing that is considered a man's. It is an ABOMINATION to God, and we should take his word seriously. Glorifying the Lord takes effort as anything worthwhile does. One way or the other, it is a choice that we all make!

<u>Sports and the female gender</u>: It is obvious that the older women are failing the younger generations by not being and teaching what they should. Our young ladies are bouncing around basketball courts, volleyball courts, soccer fields, etc.... A girl who is meek and quiet, feminine and gentle, shamefaced and busy learning how to manage a home, will not be bouncing her femininity around a court in front of everyone. Neither will she be half-dressed in a "cheer leading" outfit, while waving her arms and legs up and down in front of the crowd. Is this what God said we should teach our young ladies? God forbid! "The aged women likewise, that they be in behavior as becometh holiness, not false accusers, not given to much wine, teachers of good things; That they may teach the young women to be sober, to love their husbands, to love their children, to be discreet, chaste, keepers at home, good, obedient to their own husbands, that the word of God be not blasphemed." Titus 2:3-5.

A man in my church has had people tell him that if they decided to become a Christian, they would become Amish. It is amazing that even though the lost people he spoke with knew little about the Lord, they still identified righteous living with the Amish. What is it about them that says, "This is right" to the world? No doubt, one thing would be their modest dresses, which even a lost person associates with a holy God. Their ladies certainly are examples of modesty and humility in appearance! Could it be that lost people sense what many Christians have forgotten – that a person who claims to *know* God will be very different – including in their demeanor and dress?

One last thought from scripture, Paul proclaimed in Galatians 2:16 that a man is not justified by works before God, but by faith in Christ alone. In Ephesians 1:6 he wrote, "To the praise of the glory of his grace, wherein <u>he hath made us accepted in the beloved</u>." Paul did not contradict himself when he wrote, "Wherefore we labour, <u>that, whether present or absent, we may be accepted of him</u>..." II Corinthians 5:9. The glorious truth is that we are positionally and eternally accepted as the children of God, by faith in Christ. Yet, as God's dear children, it is important that our actions be acceptable to him. Our purpose is to glorify our Saviour with our lives. You will never be judged as an enemy, but as a child of God your works will be examined. "For we must all appear before the judgment seat of Christ; that every one may receive the things done in his body, according to that he hath done, whether it be good or bad." II Corinthians 5:10. You will never experience the flames of hell, but there are rewards that will be gained or lost based upon the daily choices you make. May the choices you make now leave you unashamed and receiving a full reward when you stand before the throne of our Lord Jesus Christ.

Though we find many of our churches are straying from the Lord, we can allow God's word to shine in and through us. Could it be that our witness to our lost friends and loved ones would be far more effective if we were more serious about knowing and pleasing the Lord? May we choose to teach our young ladies to be virtuous women by first allowing the Lord to change our hearts and lives. If there ever was a time when a godly, modest woman could make a difference in the lives of others, it's today. Will you be such a woman?

That which I see not teach thou me:
if I have done iniquity, I will do no more.

Job 34:32

Only fear the LORD, and
serve him in truth with all your heart:
for consider how great things he hath done for you.

I Samuel 12:24

BIOGRAPHICAL:

All scripture quoted from the *Authorized King James Bible*

The Sin of Bath-sheba, pgs. 3-5 Cloud, David, Mt. Carmel Publications, Portor, OK

What is fashion? article quoted from http://www.pbs.org/newshour/infocus/fashion/whatisfashion.html

What in the World Should I Wear? Corle, Cathy, Revival Fires Publishing

The Language of a Christian's Clothing: Two studies., Davis, S. M.,

The salvation testimony of Albert Benjamin Simpso, pages 99-100 Hidden Pearls, Hidden Pearls Publications © 2004

Reflections of Feminine Modesty, Laidacker, Mrs. Craig, Bloomsberg, PA, pg. 12

Noah Webster's American Dictionary of the English Language, Noah Webster's 1828